"Viva la tranquilista! Kimberly Wilson's holistic and enlightened approach offers a blueprint for living life to the fullest. Her mindful approach and creative ideas are presented in a fresh voice — like your best girlfriend giving you practical advice with a sassy twist!"

— Mary Carlomagno, author of *Secrets of Simplicity* and owner of order (www.orderperiod.com)

"*Tranquilista* is your essential guide to living a joyful, passionate, spirited life. Kimberly Wilson has a gift for creating her own inspiring magic and empowering other goddesses to do the same. *Tranquilista* shows the new way of becoming enlightened and playful, from the meditation mat to the business table."

— Leonie Allan, creator of www.goddessguidebook.com

"Kimberly Wilson's *Tranquilista* is a beautifully empowering guide for designing our lives and living fully. She lovingly guides us through ideas on how to be a soulful and compassionate entrepreneur while embracing our bliss and our beauty! I'm completely inspired by her sensitive definitions and thoughts on leaving a legacy through our daily actions and leaving a fashionable footprint on the world, all while having a good time and celebrating life. Kimberly is my new favorite guru!"

— Amy Butler, author of *Amy Butler's Midwest Modern*

"The irresistible, hip, tranquil, and oh-so-chic Kimberly Wilson is the ultimate tranquilista — a wonder woman for whom the talent of multitasking has been elevated to new heights and dimensions. Like a gorgeous Indian goddess, she must have eight arms, 'cause *she does it all* with incredible grace, elegance, compassion, wisdom, cleverness, and dazzling style — and never forgets the essential lip gloss! In her fabulous new book she generously shares all her success secrets in a very practical, yes-you-can-and-I-will-show-you-how way. I adore Kimberly. She is a true liberated woman who never compromises her femininity or her kindness for all living beings. I place her in the 'great muse' category along with Audrey and Coco."

— Sharon Gannon, coauthor of *Jivamukti Yoga*

"*Tranquilista* is the go-to guide for any woman who wants style, success, and soul in her life. Kimberly Wilson has created a life full of those things, and now she's opened up her personal book to share all her smart, sparkly, and super-inspiring secrets, girlfriend to girlfriend."

— Christine Arylo, author of *Choosing ME before WE*

TRANQUILISTA

TRANQUILISTA

Mastering the Art of
Enlightened Work and Mindful Play

KIMBERLY WILSON

New World Library
Novato, California

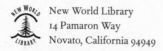

New World Library
14 Pamaron Way
Novato, California 94949

DISCLAIMER: This publication contains the opinions and ideas of its author. The advice contained herein is for informational purposes only. Please consult a medical professional before beginning any diet or exercise program. The author and publisher disclaim all responsibility for any liability, loss, risk, injury, or damage resulting from the use, proper or improper, of any of the contents of this book. Every effort has been made to ensure that the information contained in this book is complete and accurate.

Text design by Tona Pearce Myers
Cover illustrations by Anne Keenan Higgins

Library of Congress Cataloging-in-Publication Data
Wilson, Kimberly.
Tranquilista : mastering the art of enlightened work and mindful play / Kimberly Wilson.
   p.   cm.
Includes index.
ISBN 978-1-57731-672-5 (pbk. : alk. paper)
1. Hope. 2. Creative ability. 3. Lifestyles. 4. Play. I. Title.
BD216.W55 2010
650.1—dc22   2009043819

First printing, February 2010
ISBN 978-1-57731-672-5
Printed in Canada on 100% postconsumer-waste recycled paper

 New World Library is a proud member of the Green Press Initiative.

10   9   8   7   6   5   4   3   2   1

*This book is dedicated to fabulous femmes around the globe
who seek joie de vivre through spirituality, style, creative expression,
and do-gooding while leaving a sparkling legacy.*

CONTENTS

INTRODUCTION: Get Your Tranquility On

In order to be irreplaceable, one must always be different.
— COCO CHANEL

You may be wondering, "What in the world is a tranquilista?" So glad you asked! A tranquilista is a woman who embraces her many sides: spiritual (she's a tranquility-seeker), creative (loves style), and entrepreneurial (calls her own shots). She hearts fashion and philanthropy. Parties and prayer. Entertaining and enlightenment. The golden rule and layers of vintage gold bangles. She is you and she is *moi*. She is full of aspirations and always seeking inspiration. Oh, and she sparkles. Literally.

While writing my first book, *Hip Tranquil Chick: A Guide to Life on and off the Yoga Mat*, I coined the term *mindfully extravagant*. My hope was to explain embracing flair-filled must-haves such as shiny chandeliers, kitten heels, and little black dresses while also practicing yoga, meditating, caring for the environment, and be-ing a do-gooder. These two concepts may feel at odds, but when combined — like sprinkles plus icing on plain ol' vanilla cupcakes — they make even the mundane more sacred.

That's what we're doing with this book, *Tranquilista*. We're forgoing spreadsheets and stodgy office politics to forge ahead with a new way of designing our lives as self-defined entrepreneurs who care about blending balance, bliss, and beauty. Yes, even if you don't have your own business (yet) — your life is your "business." You are in charge of who you are and how you choose to live. When I use the word *entrepreneur*, I'm not referencing the standard definition of someone who finances a commercial undertaking for the sake of profit. I'm referring to today's woman who wants to leave a legacy through her daily actions, whether working for a nonprofit, launching a vegan café, or being a full-time activist. I'll show you how to do this in style through enlightened work and mindful play. I'll also show you how to stay grounded in spite of life's setbacks, ways to carve out your own unique path, and tools that will help you leave a fashionable footprint on the world. Oh, and lest I forget, ways to connect with joie de vivre along the way!

In *Tranquilista* I share stories and suggestions based on my journey as an entrepreneur since the ripe ol' age of twenty-six, a passionate yogini, a director of a nonprofit, a designer of eco-fashion, and a lover of all things fabulous. I can't wait to share the ideas with you. We'll explore the enlightened lifestyle the same way you partake in a cupcake: mix it, bake it, and decorate it with heaps of icing and sprinkles on top. A tranquilista mixes spirituality, creativity, and entrepreneurship in varied amounts to bake the perfect concoction that will help her attain her individual dreams and desires while making a positive impact. I explore these three key ingredients of the tranquilista philosophy in depth throughout this book, but let's take a quick look at them now:

Spirituality is your foundation for focusing within, growing, and giving back — it's your how-to for living life fully and mindfully. Commune with nature. Live your values. Be a self-proclaimed do-gooder. Go green. Set up an altar. Name and go after your aspirations. Meditate. Connect with your spirit daily. Explore your dreams. Exude a spark that inspires others.

Creativity is where you shine as an individual. Think of your life as an artist's masterpiece. Find inspiration in the mundane.

Explore DIY projects. Be unconventional. Dress with panache. Revel in indulgent self-care. Color outside the lines daily. Paint your nails with Lincoln Park after Dark. Fill your body with greens and whole grains. Do yoga. Write a blog. Do more yoga. Throw lavish parties for a cause. Be delectably and uniquely you in word, thought, and action.

Entrepreneurship is all about carving out your own special spot in this world. Find an opportunity and make your mark, whether you launch your own business, stay at home with tots, or work for a Fortune 500 company. Innovate. Create an experience uniquely you. Cultivate nurturing relationships. Teach. Save for retirement. Be your brand. Engage in social media. Become an expert. Grow organically. Diversify. Manage your time and energy. Leave your legacy. Consciously choose what you want to convey to the world.

When blended in your unique formula, these three ingredients ensure that you will live in a way that shines, makes a difference, encourages others, and helps you grow beyond your wildest dreams. *Tranquilista* serves up scoops of inspiration in eight sensational, sustainable sections. These are best read in order, but if you're eager to jump to a topic that feels supersexy and is further along the path, give in to your desire guilt-free. However, the book is set up to cover the groundwork first, and each piece builds on the last, so, *s'il vous plaît*, return to the earlier sections before relocating the book from your bedside to your built-ins. Oh, and note the "Savvy Sources" strewn throughout. These give you an opportunity to explore a topic (and yourself) further.

This book is packed with life-changing gems. Sure, sounds dramatic, but who doesn't like a small dose of drama from time to time? Don a comfy chenille robe. Put Carla Bruni on shuffle. Keep your embossed damask journal nearby at all times. Lie back in your toile-covered chaise. Have a cup of tea (or flute of Veuve Cliquot) in hand, and get ready for an enlightened and extravagant ride.

TRANQUILISTA MANIFESTO

I, _____, promise to

- connect to my spiritual core daily.
- access my aspirations seasonally and create aligned action steps.
- be an activist for causes close to my heart and do good every day.
- express my creativity daily and replenish my creative spark weekly.
- exude my signature style in a way that helps my inner spirit shine.
- start something that aligns with my values, intentions, and passions.
- build a brand with authenticity and a focus on community.
- expand organically, strategically, and compassionately.

PART 1. MIX MINDFULNESS

Ingredients for Tranquility

1. SASSY SPIRITUALITY

Spirit is an invisible force made visible in all life.

— MAYA ANGELOU

To start your journey as a tranquilista, let's get grounded and connect to your spiritual side, the foundation of enlightened living. I'll help you take your spirituality to the street by serving up real-world tips rooted in Eastern philosophy, ways to live mindfully despite your pesky BlackBerry, and my favorite can't-live-without tools to ensure oodles of calm.

The "act of being mindful" is a grandiose phrase for simply being in the moment. Ever notice that most of our suffering comes from rehashing the past, worrying about the future, or wishing things could be different than they are in the present? Being a mindful maven is not about perfection; it's about being fully and completely present with what is: the raw, the juicy, the not-so-juicy, the letdowns, and the celebrations.

MODERN-DAY MINDFULNESS TIPS

Mindfulness is not something to practice only at church or the yoga studio, but is an important trait to adorn yourself with at all times. Ever had those moments of opening your mouth and immediately regretting what you've said? How about replying to an email and hitting "send" in a flash, only to wish you could crawl into a cyberspace hole afterward? What about forgetting to say thank you after being given a thoughtful token? Ever been snippy to the girl at the counter who isn't making your soy chai latte quickly enough? These are everyday moments of mind*less*ness of the sort that we're all guilty of from time to time. You're reading this book because you crave something different, a state of being kind, compassionate, fabulous, and giving. Following are my favorite modes of invoking mindfulness while on the go.

Say a Passion-Filled Prayer

When I grew up in small-town Oklahoma, giving thanks for food and requesting that loved ones be watched over (and saved) was the norm before meals. My prayers have evolved since those early days. Prayer offers the chance to connect to something larger than ourselves. I derive solace from bringing my hands together and bowing to something or someone else. This simple act is done regularly at the end of most yoga classes and is a sacred way of acknowledging the spirits of those around you. My beau reminds me that he was smitten after I did the hands-together-nod at the end of our first date. It is a very humbling action to bow to another being, especially an omnipresent God or Goddess. This simple gesture can be a reverent way to acknowledge your interconnectedness with other beings and even the unknown.

Bathe in Affirmations

Ever notice that the little voice inside your head may not always be your biggest fan? Self-doubt is sure to creep in despite your best efforts to exorcise the nasty demon. Don't worry; it's not just you. Even the most celebrated actresses and writers say they battle this same issue. Lingering fears of not being as good at something as others think you are often lead to a larger fear of being "found out."

PRAYER PARTY

Prayer is not asking. It is a longing of the soul. It is daily admission of one's weakness. It is better in prayer to have a heart without words than words without a heart.

— MOHANDAS GANDHI

Still filled with Catholic guilt? Not quite sure how to make this connection with the Divine as a willing adult participant? Take time to communicate with a spirit that beckons you, whether it be Buddha, Jesus, or Elvis. Come to a comfortable place, carve out some time, and get into position. Prepare by lighting a candle, fasting, ringing a bell, or bowing to your altar — whatever resonates for you. Try a cross-legged seated pose, kneel near a window, or simply lie still on your bed. Create your own ritual. Find your own way to pray — it's your party. Begin the prayer by singing, reading, reciting a favorite quote, or lowering your head. Express gratitude. Ask for courage. Send good thoughts to others. Seek solace. Share your thoughts. It's like journal writing aloud. Finish with a bow, an "amen," a ring of the bell, or by blowing out the candle. Voilà, you've had your own prayer party. Rinse and repeat as needed.

5

The way I combat those not-so-positive voices is with affirmations — short, pithy, positive statements made in the present tense. You may ask, "Really, I'm supposed to say things like 'I am beautiful,' 'I can do anything,' 'I am a successful writer'?" Indeed you are!

There is a whole café built around affirmations in the San Francisco Bay Area called Café Gratitude. Every item on the menu is an affirmation. It's inspiring just to place an order. I'm a big fan of their "I am bold." If you're in the area, why not try their "I am happy" or "I am peaceful"? Rather than simply ordering vegan nachos or pizza, the café ensures that you will take a moment to repeat a positive affirmation. Customers are asked: "What are you grateful for today?"

Next time self-doubt comes for a visit, ignore it and instead start your day, meeting, or event on a positive note by reciting the mantra "I can do anything" and watching what transpires. Your mind will quickly catch up with your mouth.

Pen Your Thoughts

Tap into your spiritual and creative sides through this time-tested tradition. Journal writing has been an important part of my life since the wise young age of eight. Writing your innermost thoughts on paper allows for reflection, the chance to capture the moment, and a private space where you can spill how you really feel without concerns about grammar, tear- or ink stains, or losing a friend. Do you find yourself complaining about the same thing repeatedly? Do you see patterns in your comments about relationships? If so, this is the perfect realm in which to explore ways to make changes. Do you notice a negative tone during certain months? Maybe that's the time to dash off to a warmer climate for some much-needed R&R.

In the morning before your coffee kicks in, start writing whatever comes to the surface. This allows you to start your day with a clean slate. You can also do your writing before bed as a tool for reflection. Others use their journals to recap the day with basic information like where they brunched and what movies they saw. Some write to diffuse pent-up emotions they dare not share publicly. Over the years I have found that the volume of my journal writing increases during challenging times of transition, such as breakups or moves. *How* you use your journal doesn't really matter; just using it is the point.

I find that handy phrases to jump-start my writing can be

6

helpful tools on days when staring at the blank page seems overwhelming. For example, try:

Today I am feeling _____.
I am most happy when _____.
I am bothered by _____.
I really want _____.
or
I continue to struggle with _____.

SAVVY SOURCE FOR FURTHER EXPLORATION

Wreck This Journal, by Keri Smith

These small springboards can uncover some interesting material.

Assume Your Meditation Position

Ah, the simple act of *being* — so much harder than *doing*. Why is sitting still and focusing on our breath such a tricky endeavor? For the girl-on-the-go, this single act can bring an enormous amount of tranquility. Meditation encourages us to slow down, empty our overactive minds, and provide rest for our bodies. One teacher describes the benefit of meditation as the chance to have space between a stimulus and a response. The practice of meditation allows us to be less reactive. Remember this tip the next time you receive an unpleasant email. Take deep breaths, create space before reacting, and notice that you can retrain yourself to more compassionately handle situations that push your buttons. The benefits may not seem obvious immediately after you've sat on your hot-pink cushion, but hopefully they will be apparent in your words and actions post-meditation. You, your colleagues, and beau will thank you for this newfound spaciousness and your thoughtfulness.

Now, let's go through a simple seated meditation together. Gather these accoutrements: a kitchen timer, chime, meditation cushion or firm pillow to elevate your hips, and (optional) incense or a peony-scented soy candle. Sit comfortably cross-legged on the front edge of your cushion with your hips elevated above your knees (or in a chair), light your incense or candle, set the kitchen timer for

7

SAVVY SOURCE FOR FURTHER EXPLORATION

Unplug for an Hour, a Day, or a Weekend, by Sharon Salzberg

ten minutes, and sound the chime. Rest your hands on your thighs with the palms facing down, let your elbows rest comfortably, and allow your eyes to close. When the kitchen timer goes off, open your eyes, do a few gentle stretches, and prepare to emerge from your meditation more grounded.

Get Your Gratitude On

Recently I was asked if I ever take a moment to reflect on what I have accomplished. I was taken aback by the brazenness of the question. Who has time to observe such things when we are always in forward motion and looking toward the next thing? I confess, that was my *initial* reaction. Now I see the question as a call

8

BUT WHAT DO I THINK ABOUT DURING MEDITATION?

The million-dollar question! We're not just working hard *not* to think. The idea is to practice *being*. Simply sit and experience your breath and all the sensations floating about your body. Observe your mind jumping from thought to thought like a monkey in a forest traveling quickly from limb to limb. Practice being the observer of this monkey, and see if you can gradually slow the monkey down. Maybe settle it onto a tree limb to stay a while.

There is no goal. Really. The point is to slow down, be still, and focus within. Some sessions will be blissful, while others will feel like absolute torture. Your feet may fall asleep. You may wonder if the kitchen timer broke. And your mind will continue being, well, monkeylike. The key is to continually return to your meditation cushion, to develop a consistent practice. I strive to start each day with at least ten minutes of meditation, and I have found it to be a critical foundation for my morning.

to action, to focus on gratitude. Moving forward is important for our aspirations; gratitude is important for our souls.

Each day during the next week, list ten items you are grateful for that day. Here's a selection from my recent list written during a nature getaway:

> I am grateful for the tiny frog hopping on the sidewalk.
> I am grateful for the sound of pouring rain.
> I am grateful for the four deer in the front yard.
> I am grateful for my disconnection from the Internet and the forced internal connection.

Explore the mundane, explore the exotic. Honor the beauty that crosses your path each and every day, such as flowering, scented trees and bushes, a fallow daffodil pushing up from the barren earth, artwork in the office, or colorful fruit displays at the grocery store. Acknowledge what you accomplish daily, even if it's simply getting out of bed or getting to the office on time in clean clothes. Otherwise, our mindfulness is stuck on moving toward the future, rather than being in the present and encouraging ourselves along the way. Go ahead, give yourself a pat or, better yet, a massage.

9

Celebrate Scents

"The more scent, the better" is my frequent mantra. I'm like a kid in a candy store when I walk into highly aromatic settings such as LUSH and the Body Shop. Most evenings I have a few scented candles burning, along with sticks of incense. Lavender essential oil is a must-have, and I carry it in my bag to dab onto my wrists or sniff at a moment's notice. Scents make us happy, hence the term aroma*therapy*. Scents have incredibly therapeutic benefits. I highly recommend you have on hand a few essential oils that can enhance a mood:

LAVENDER. My go-to scent. This oil is all about relaxation. It has antiseptic and anti-inflammatory properties, plus it helps ward off mosquitoes. Add dried buds to pillows, sachets, and cards sent via snail mail. Great for cooking, drinking (a lavender-infused TranquilTini recipe is forthcoming), and bathing too.

SWEET ORANGE. Perfect for studying. This citrusy scent uplifts and detoxifies. It also assists with fighting colds and cleaning.

LEMONGRASS. Smells heavenly and is used in cooking. Great for reducing headaches, helping with jet lag, and soothing respiratory infections. An overall yummy tonic for the nervous system.

CLARY SAGE. I've been told this is *the* must-have scent. It does it all. It's an antidepressant, an antiseptic, digestive and reproductive help, and a muscle relaxant all in one. Smells a bit nutty, and offers lots of power.

PEPPERMINT. This delightful oil reminds me of the holidays and is great for a quick pick-me-up. Promotes alertness. Good for digestion and decongestion.

10

SAVVY SOURCE FOR FURTHER EXPLORATION

The Aromatherapy Bible: The Definitive Guide to Using Essential Oils, by Gill Farrer-Halls

Don't forget scented candles to help set a mood and elevate your own. Choose soy over paraffin, essential oils over fragrance oils, and hemp wicks over paraffin wicks. Reuse the glass containers to hold paperclips, tea lights, candy, or business cards. All this ensures you're earth friendly while indulging in tranquility.

Create Space

In our busy lives, the possibility of finding a sense of spaciousness can seem as far-fetched as writing a novel in one day. You may find yourself scheduled from sunup to snooze time, and then wonder what in the world you did, despite the fact that you were going ninety miles a minute all day long. Sound familiar? Mindfulness is most easily found within spaciousness. Yes, even scheduled spaciousness. I'm such a planner that I've had to literally trick myself into finding space in my calendar by scheduling downtime. This block of time allows me to take a step back, regroup, and make sure that I'm still on track. Sometimes it allows me a luxuriant nap or a long soak in the tub. You can still be productive, accomplish your aspirations, and take a moment for yourself. The key is to make it happen.

Can you picture always-late "Lucy" who rushes in to the office looking disheveled, breathing heavily from running, and apologizing that traffic was bad (yet again)? Lucy is an example of a person who lacks spaciousness. You may be blushing because you recognize yourself. We've all been there. We just don't want to continue being *that* girl. Exude mindfulness by arriving a few minutes early — be prepared, account for possible traffic or parking concerns, and be organized. As Maya Angelou reminds us, "You did then what you knew how to do. When you knew better, you did better." Do better by creating some sacred space in your daily routine.

Catch Your Dreams

We've explored heaps of tips for becoming more mindful while conscious. Now let's touch on our unconscious dreaming state. Sure, it may sound like a bit of a stretch, but our dreams are powerful and full of interesting connections to what we may not yet be ready to face in reality. Psychoanalyst Carl Jung believed that dreams have the potential to teach us something about ourselves. I believe they can be powerful pathways to what is brewing within.

Start by keeping a pen and paper on your bedside table. This is perfect for recording those almost-asleep-but-thought-of-something-else moments, along with your groggy early-morning recollections of your dreams. We are quick to forget our dreams once we get going, so we must capture them immediately. You may not know why you consistently dream about certain things or people, but by recording dreams regularly, you will begin to see patterns and can explore them more deeply with the help of books, Jungian analysts, or your friends. Start a dream exploration club.

If you're looking for an answer to something you're struggling with, try asking a question before you fall asleep, and let your subconscious mull it over while you slumber. Remember, all answers are within — sometimes they just need a little coaxing to come out.

Rock an Altar

An altar can be a small or grandiose setup of your favorite inspirational items, a special spot to get your spiritual self going at the start of your day, before heading to bed, or anytime in between. For as long as I can remember, I have had a nook to host images of my beloveds, candles, incense, flowers, plants, sacred books, and deities. My altar has been everything from a desk to a bench to a mantel to a windowsill, and currently it's my hearth. I have Ganesha (remover of obstacles), Lakshmi (goddess of abundance), and Saraswati (goddess of creativity) prominently displayed alongside a big, glass Buddha head. A vase filled with incense sticks. Tons of candles. A kitchen timer. A meditation cushion. Bamboo stalks. And framed photos of my beau, pug, and BFF. Even when I travel, I take a selection of the above to ensure a homey, spiritual vibe while in unknown territory. Let your altar be a comfortable spot where you can sit and reflect, meditate, or decompress while you're surrounded by a few of your favorite things.

Additional ideas on what to include on your altar are tokens from your travels, postcards, handwritten letters, artwork, quotes, seashells, stones, and crystals. Why not frame pictures of spiritual teachers to display on your altar? I've often joked that I want to frame photos of

SAVVY SOURCE FOR FURTHER EXPLORATION

Altars: Bringing Sacred Shrines into Your Everyday Life, by Denise Linn

12

Madonna and Gloria Steinem for my altar. Whatever you choose, or whoever inspires you, let your altar be uniquely yours, even if you want to frame an unapologetic rock star.

Find Your Inner Nature Girl

Some tranquilistas find God at church, others in the great outdoors. Ever been on a gondola traveling up one of the snowcapped Rocky Mountain peaks? I swear *that* is a spiritual experience. When I lived in Colorado for a season postcollege, I was awestruck every time I donned my gear and headed up the mountain to partake in an exhilarating ride back down. There is truly something magical to be found within nature.

Take a bike ride through your local park. Pack your lunch and head to a city park to dine mid-workday. Go camping — yes, car camping counts. Enjoy a Sunday afternoon hike or stroll through your nearby state park. Take a fall foliage tour through the Northeast. Rent a cabin in the country as often as you can. Snowshoe by moonlight. Nap under a big oak tree. Go rock climbing. Splash around at the beach. Walk through Muir Woods near San Francisco and breathe in the best-smelling air I've ever come across. Pitch a tent near a redwood tree in the Northwest and feel your city-living problems dissolve. Nature has a calming effect that can help keep us, and our trite everyday dramas, in perspective.

Go Totally *Tonglen*

In Buddhism, *tonglen* is a lovingkindness- and compassion-filled practice that is easily done on the bus, at the bank, or in a boardroom. It translates as "giving and receiving." Here's the skinny: when you see someone suffering, or you know someone who is suffering, practice breathing in their pain and sending out love. Visualize their suffering (that of a crying baby, a tense boss, or a distraught colleague) as a dark cloud that you draw in as you

SAVVY SOURCE FOR FURTHER EXPLORATION

Good Medicine: How to Turn Pain into Compassion with Tonglen Meditation, by Pema Chödrön

inhale, and send out loving compassion in the form of white light as you exhale. Think of your breath as a filter. In practicing *tonglen*, we don't hold onto their pain, but rather we act as a catalyst. This has the capacity to change your connection to, and empathy for, others — especially the ones who have a tendency to push your buttons.

Explore Chic Chants

Chanting is a common spiritual practice used to evoke emotion and/or acknowledge the Divine. As a lover of *kirtan* (call-and-response chanting of words or phrases), I want to share a few of my favorites in case you'd like to tone your vocal cords and sing along.

14

LOKAH SAMASTA SUKINO BHAVANTU. Sharon Gannon of Jivamukti Yoga translates this as "May all beings everywhere be happy and free. May the thoughts, words, and actions of my own life contribute in some way to that happiness and to that freedom for all." I recite this chant during most yoga classes I teach, and when I'm struggling with anger or other negative emotions. I've even contemplated having it tattooed on my back (in fancy script, of course). Sure, that was a fleeting contemplation. But this mantra serves as a reminder to ensure that what I do affects others in a positive way.

OM. This is considered the original sound in the universe and is one of the most powerful mantras. Chanting this sound encourages a connection between us and the world and all of those around us. A beautiful reminder of our interconnectedness to others, nature, and beyond.

OM MANI PADME HUM. This beautiful Buddhist chant, sung divinely by singer Deva Premal, means "The precious jewel is in the lotus.

All that needs to be known dwells inside your own heart." I appreciate this reminder to recognize that all answers lie within. Why search outside when there is so much beauty and knowledge to be found in your very own spirit?

AMAZING GRACE

Amazing grace. How sweet the sound
That saved a wretch like me.
I once was lost, but now am found;
Was blind, but now I see.
'Twas grace that taught my heart to fear,
And grace my fears relieved;
How precious did that grace appear
The hour I first believed.

This song has been popular among Christians and non-Christians and has served as a theme song for human rights supporters throughout centuries. It reminds us of our connection to divine grace and recognizes a higher power.

Find a Must-Have Morning Ritual

I once asked my blog readers for feedback on how they start their days. I was awed by the response. For years I've leapt out of bed and headed straight to the computer. Yep, even on the weekends. Even though each morning after logging on I contemplated crawling back under my covers for more shut-eye, I was inspired by the bliss-filled morning rituals that readers shared with me. Thanks to their ideas, I've made some great strides in launching tranquility at the start of the day. Let me give you some examples:

Get your yoga on. Start the day with yummy stretches, such as sun salutations.

Enjoy a moment of silence. Set your kitchen timer (or

15

download a free meditation chime for your Mac) for
ten minutes and just be.

Savor getting ready. Rather than rushing out the door,
leave ample time for primping, sitting down for
breakfast, and writing in your journal.

Pack your lunch (and snacks). Take this time to ensure
that you're feeling healthy and fulfilled throughout
the day.

Stimulate your mind. Let some thought-provoking head-
lines or a favorite inspirational book percolate through
your mind.

The key is to set your intention for your day. Let your start be
serene, strategic, and therapeutic to your spirit — not rushed,
chaotic, and stressful. This will help set the tone for what will unfold and ground you — much different than rushing out the door
with wet hair, juggling your breakfast and espresso.

Adopt Eight Yogic Steps for Mindful Mavens

As a yoga teacher and practitioner for over a decade, I love
to refer back to the basic tenets of yoga, outlined by the sage
Patanjali in the Indian sacred text the *Yoga Sutras*, to guide my
spiritual side. My favorite version of the Sutras is the first trans-
lation by a woman, Nischala Joy Devi, called *The Secret Power of
Yoga*. It's a great read if you'd like to learn more about these ancient teachings from a fellow femme's perspective.

We all need some sort of road map to help us stay the course
and make minor adjustments along the way. The following steps,
outlined in the Sutras as the eight limbs of yoga, are great everyday guidelines for mindful bliss.

YAMAS. These five guidelines give insights into how to act toward
others, and they promote nonviolence, truthfulness, moderation,
greedlessness, and not stealing. An example of nonviolence is to

make lifestyle choices that lessen your carbon footprint, such as riding your bike to work, eating fruits and vegetables in season, carrying a reusable bag, and turning off the water while brushing your teeth.

NIYAMAS. These five guidelines focus on how you treat yourself, and they promote purity, contentment, austerity, self-study, and letting go. An example of self-study involves focusing within to recognize patterns, review expectations, and practice acceptance of what is. By doing so, you become able to better understand who you are and why you react the way you do, and to accept situations beyond your control. Let go of that dirty word *should*.

ASANAS (poses). Practicing poses, such as down dog, cobra, and lion's pose, is what, in the West, we commonly refer to as yoga. The physical practice of yoga is a great way to still the mind and awaken the body. Use your body as a catalyst for change by observing all the sensations that transpire in challenging poses or challenging situations in life. Our bodies hold keys for amazing transformations.

17

PRANAYAMA (breath work). Breath control is a powerful tool for use during our daily lives. Notice how your breath becomes shallow when you're on deadline or waiting in a long line. Take deep, full breaths to induce a calming effect and cleanse and balance your nervous system. Take ten deep, full breaths before heading in for your annual review, and notice the powerful effect. My three favorite *prana* practices are unveiled in the upcoming section on breath.

PRATYAHARA (withdrawal of senses). This concept encourages us to avoid reacting to everything around us. Picture yourself calm, collected, and compassionate in the middle of a mall on the day after Thanksgiving. Embrace this step in chaotic situations such as family reunions, a fire alarm, or an overreacting colleague. Release all the distractions around you to become fully present with what is happening.

DHARANA (concentration). This is the ability to be completely in the moment and focused on only one thing. Use mantras, breath, images, or even candles to help bring yourself into focus. When interacting with others, practice being fully present with them — no texting, no watching who else may be walking by, no checking your watch. The Zen Buddhist monk and peace activist Thich Nhat Hanh reminds us: "The most precious gift we can offer others is our presence. When mindfulness embraces those we love, they will bloom like flowers." Help others bloom.

18

DHYANA (meditation). Turn inward, release the mind, and focus on just being in that moment. Much easier said than done, but it is a critical addition to the physical practice of yoga. It is said that yogis first began practicing their fabulous yoga poses to prepare their bodies for meditation. During your busy day, secure at least five minutes to sit still, focus on your breath, and let go of outside distractions. This assists you with being more proactive and less reactive in daily life. Very helpful — especially if you tend to be a drama queen!

SAVVY SOURCE FOR FURTHER EXPLORATION

Flow: The Psychology of Optimal Experience, by Mihaly Csikszentmihalyi

SAMADHI (true bliss). This is the experience of wholeness when you are in the flow and feeling connected to all. Think inner peace, bliss, and overall freedom. This step is considered the ultimate experience, where you have control over distractions. Reflect on times when you feel completely in the zone, when you lose track of time and feel perfectly at peace.

Connect with Your Breath

One of the best ways to stay mindful in the moment is to connect fully with your breath. Inhale. Exhale. Conscious breathing is a must-have add-on to combat daily stressors. I've included here the how-to scoop on three of my favorite breathing practices: three-part yogic breath, alternate-nostril breath, and *kapalabhati* breath. These little gems come in handy in all situations — from giving a presentation to ending a relationship to handling rush hour traffic.

Sure, you may have to excuse yourself from a public place to do some of the breaths, but in a matter of a few moments you can experience bliss. Follow these simple steps and enjoy having tranquility within reach — unless you are feeling stuffy, sneezy, and cold-ridden. If you're suffering from sinus congestion, wait to try them until you feel well and can breathe fully through both nostrils.

Start each breath in a comfortable cross-legged seated position or at the edge of your chair.

Three-Part Yogic Breath

Feeling a little out of sync or stressed? Begin by taking a few deep, full breaths. Count to four as you draw your breath in through your nose. Count to four as you exhale through your nose. Soften your jaw and unclench your teeth. Soften your tongue and let it rest at the bottom of your mouth. After a few rounds of four-count breaths, draw your breath into your belly, up into your lungs, and then your chest. Now exhale from the top down, beginning with your chest, then lungs, and then belly. Picture yourself filling your body as you would fill a glass with water — you fill the bottom, middle, and top, then you pour it out from the top, middle, and bottom. Visualize your cares and concerns releasing along with your exhalation. This simple breathing technique can do wonders to create calm in a challenging situation.

The three-part yogic breath will assist you in overcoming the body's automatic fight-or-flight response. It also offers you an opportunity to turn within, slow down, and recharge at any time throughout your day. Breathe deeply and feel fabulous.

Alternate-Nostril Breath

Craving balance and a state of calm? Place your right middle and index fingers on the point between your eyebrows so that your thumb, ring, and pinky fingers are free. Close your right nostril with your thumb. Inhale deeply through your left nostril. Close your left nostril with your ring finger, release your right nostril, and exhale through your right nostril. Inhale through your right nostril and then close your right nostril to exhale through your left nostril. Inhale through your left nostril and then close your left nostril to exhale through your right nostril. Continue this back-and-forth pattern until it feels natural. Then increase the length of your inhale to a count of four, five, or six, and exhale for the same length of time, so that your breath becomes long, deep, and smooth. Alternate-nostril breathing balances both sides of the brain and assists with calming your mind and nervous system.

Kapalabhati Breath

This cleansing, energizing breath is a forced exhalation with an automatic inhalation and is commonly called the "Breath of Fire." Rest your hand on your belly and send a powerful exhalation through your nose. Move your belly like a piston, with a snap-like motion. Try this a few times, focusing on your exhalation until you get a rhythm going. You can adjust the pace to be very quick — and the breath sounds like a choo-choo train — or slow and steady. Take thirty Breaths of Fire and, over time, build to one hundred. Practice this breath regularly to detox your system and energize your mind.

SPIRITUAL STYLE

I've offered many tools here to assist you with connecting to Spirit. Some of these practices you may already do, others may be occasional indulgences, and some suggestions may feel too far-fetched for you to try. The key at this stage is to develop a way to live without regrets. Do your best every day. And, ultimately, ensure that your thoughts, words, and actions make a positive contribution to other people. Does this sound too big? Well, it is big. Your life can have a powerful effect on those around you. Make sure it is a mindful, loving, compassionate one.

MODEL MUSE

The lovely Sera Beak is bringing a redvolution to the world. As a Harvard-trained divinity scholar, she helps women find the divine spark and delicious truth in spirituality. Her book, *The Red Book: A Deliciously Unorthodox Approach to Igniting Your Divine Spark*, is full of tips on grazing the spiritual buffet, 1,001 ways of giving prayer a makeover, embracing your sexuality, asking tough questions, trusting your intuition, and more. I attended her workshop at the National Cathedral in Washington, DC, and must say that her passion for spirituality is catchy and suffuses her every sentence. Her potty mouth and down-to-earth approach to modern-day spirituality kept us laughing and reflecting at the same time. Learn about Sera at Serabeak.com, and listen to my podcast interview with her at Tranquilitydujour.com.

2. ALMIGHTY ASPIRATIONS

*The journey of a thousand miles begins with a
single step.*

— LAO-TZU

When I was a tween I thumbed through *Seventeen* magazine and wondered why I didn't have the coordinated bedroom, well-coiffed hair, adoring boyfriend, or stylish accoutrements that all the happy models seemed to possess. As an awkward girl living in Oklahoma and longing for all things fabulous, I had no idea that the world was my oyster. Unfortunately, they didn't teach us that in middle school. Over the years, I have learned how to make things happen by setting goals, taking action steps, making regular assessments, and possessing loads of gusto. Throughout this section we'll explore how these tools translate to achieving your aspirations. Now, close your shimmering eyelids and let me take your well-manicured hand. This is where the magic happens!

STATE OF THE UNION

As one schoolteacher used to tell me, if you know where you're heading, but don't know where you are, you're already lost. It's important to take stock regularly (I prefer to do so with the change of seasons, on my birthday, and at the start of the new year) and determine how fulfilled you are in the various areas of your life. Does your job still feel like a good fit? How about your close relationships? What about where you live? Does your level of physical activity feel right? You get the gist. Let's do a mini-assessment of how satisfied you are with how you spend your 24/7s.

Lifestyle Reflection

Pull out your journal or a blank sheet of paper. Take a moment to ponder the top ten things that take up your time during an average week: family obligations, day job, synagogue, school, moonlighting, community activities, online surfing, TV watching, pet care, yoga, shopping, volunteering, maintenance (manis, pedis, massage, hair), cooking, reading, networking, a favorite hobby, daydreaming, and so on. Don't judge them; just list your top ten along the left side of your paper.

On the right side of your paper, list the top ten ways you *would like* to spend your time: quilting, knitting, writing, reading, volunteering, building a business, meal planning, taking hot baths, caring for a child, advancing your career, blogging, meditating, spending time among like-minded friends, and so on.

Now rate the ten items on the left side on a scale of 1 (lowest) to 5 (highest) according to how satisfied you are with the amount of your day they take up. Upon reflection you may realize that you are spending a lot more time with sitcoms and email than on your beloved beading or on building your business. How many items are on both your left and right list? Do you see ways to merge the two lists? Are there items on your left list that can be cut down and/or replaced with items from your right list? This activity allows you to reflect on how you are actually spending your time and whether it aligns with how you want to be spending your time.

By assessing where your 24/7s go, you can continue to explore your levels of satisfaction and your dreams for something bigger. How you spend your time speaks to your values. Sometimes you're proactive, other times you're reactive. This stage is all about becoming more proactive to ensure that you leave a magical mark on this world. If your left and right lists are not aligned, read on. If they *are* aligned, good for you. Feel free to skip ahead to "Setting Goals."

Change Reflection

So your ideal and your current reality are involved in a mini tug-of-war? This is not uncommon. Frankly, it's the norm. After all, we are all works in progress. My goal is to help you heal the divide so that you have more congruency between your ideal and actual use of time. You can't wait until retirement to create the garden you've always wanted, build the country bed-and-breakfast with a vineyard vista, or travel to sacred temples across the globe. The time is now. Pull out your journal and explore the following questions.

1. Where am I spending time and energy now?
2. How do I want to be spending my time and energy?
3. How can I cut back on some of the time and energy drains in my life right now?
4. How can I spend some of my time and energy the way I really want to, starting immediately?

SETTING GOALS

Ever look at other people's lives and think they must have been granted a courtesy pass from the Abundance Goddess? Some people make success look very easy, but it rarely happens without a lot of planning and persistence. If you want to make something happen, you can't just wish it so. You have to begin planting seeds now to move toward your tranquility-filled dream life. Oh, and you can't keep digging them up along the way because they aren't growing fast enough — believe me, I've tried. Patience is a virtue, my dear, especially when it comes to achieving your aspirations.

Goals are what you want to achieve in your life, and they are incredibly personal. Some people never think to write them down, much less share them with others. However, studies show that those who take these extra steps are much more likely to make their dreams a reality. Of course, many people jump on the goal-setting bandwagon at New Year's, but what about the other 364 days? It's important to get clear on your goals so that you can take action daily that will help you achieve them. *Daily* is the operative word.

To give you an example of setting a goal, carving out a plan, and being patient, let's review my goal of writing a book. In 2000, I worked with a writing coach who gave me a short list of classic writing books to read — you know the ones, *Bird by Bird* and *If You Want to Write*. To figure out an overarching theme for the book, I collected images of subjects that appealed to me, and we posted them on a big bulletin board. Even with all those images, I still didn't have my "aha" moment.

So, I began to dabble during the next couple of years by writing articles for local newsletters and small publications. Finally a lightbulb went off in 2003 when I got the idea for a book on yoga for the modern girl. Observing the growing number of yoga books on the shelves, but realizing there were none about the city-dwelling diva living *la vida* yoga, I decided that was my story. I coined the book concept "hip yoga chick" and took a local book-writing course for aspiring authors to hone my idea. In 2004, I began working my way through Michael Larsen's bible, *How to Write a Book Proposal*, and completed an online program on book writing. After many months I finished my proposal, researched like-minded agents, and sent query letters to a dozen of them.

In late 2004 I heard from an enthusiastic agent who said my book proposal was the nicest looking — and smelling (because of the enclosed tea bag) — she had received. I'd sent the proposal in a polka-dot file folder with an illustration of a girl doing yoga glued to the outside. Inside were colorful tabs breaking up the proposal and appendices — all in my signature font. I included promotional materials on my studio, a magnet, and a bag of Breathe Deep Yogi Tea on the inner panels.

Luckily, my agent and I found an equally enthusiastic publisher in late 2005. I had six months to write and edit the book. Voilà, *Hip Tranquil Chick* was released in late 2006. By including the word *tranquil* in the title, I was able to associate the book with my businesses: my yoga studio, Tranquil Space; clothing line, TranquiliT; and nonprofit, Tranquil Space Foundation.

TIME LINE TO HIP TRANQUIL CHICKNESS

2000: Decided to write a book; began working with a writing coach.
2001: Began writing articles for small publications.
2003: Determined the theme for the book.
2004: Began writing my book proposal and got a book agent.
2005: Got a publisher.
2006: Launched Hiptranquilchick.com; *Hip Tranquil Chick* hit the shelves for the holidays.

The time line above illustrates the time, effort, and patience it took *moi* to accomplish one goal. Six years. Many people believe there is a book inside them, yet only a small percentage of them bring that book to fruition, and still fewer are picked up by an agent or publisher. Granted, some goals can be more instantaneous, such as cleaning your closet; others take time and even more patience. The key is to break your goals down into action steps so that the goal itself doesn't feel overwhelming.

Let's take a moment to capture and clarify your goals. What are your short-term and longer-term goals? Get specific on what you want to have done by the end of three months, next year, and five years. Jot down at least three goals for each of these points on

27

your time line and attach them to your boudoir mirror so you can't forget about them. They can be personal or professional goals, it doesn't matter. Look for harmony and continual growth in every area of your life, whatever hat you wear in that area: friend, partner, boss, activist, employee, mother, sister, daughter, philanthropist.

Here's where it gets fun. Write your goals in the present tense as an affirmation. For example, if the goal is to be an interior designer in five years, your affirmation should be "I am becoming a talented interior designer." The key is to start believing it yourself. Fake it 'til you make it! I learned this motto in ninth-grade speech class when I was nervous about my first public talk in front of my peers. You have to step up to the podium, be bold, exude confidence, and harness the potential you have within. I continue to recall this motto when self-doubt creeps in. Now, go ahead, give each of your goals an affirmation.

Take Action Steps

This is where the rubber meets the road. You've got your goals; now let's figure out how to get you to the final destination. It all starts with breaking big goals down into manageable, bite-sized action steps. If you don't break them into these little nuggets, goals can seem too far away or, even worse for the psyche, unattainable. I believe you can accomplish whatever you set out to do if you follow these steps (and add a sprinkle of joie de vivre). Whatever you want to call it, zest is a must-have ingredient when bringing any goal to life. Without it, life has a continual fog obscuring your full vista of possibility.

Begin by choosing one of your three-month goals. Note three action steps that can help you accomplish this goal. Declaring a goal isn't enough. You must see that it's possible to attain. For example, take the big-picture goal and lay out the action steps and associated time lines necessary to make it happen. Ask yourself,

"What daily steps will help me achieve this goal?" Say your three-month goal is to cut out coffee, and you currently drink two to three cups per day. Your action steps may include (1) slowly weaning yourself down to one cup per day within six weeks, (2) beginning to drink green tea, and (3) removing coffee completely by week twelve and replacing your morning cup of joe with a pot of fragrant jasmine tea. Sound doable? Let's keep going.

Now list your three one-year goals. How can you bring these to life? Maybe your one-year goal is to open a flower shop. Who wouldn't want to be surrounded by fresh-cut peonies and stargazer lilies all day? Three action steps may include (1) information gathering: read all you can on running your own business and, in particular, the floral market, (2) market research: find a location, flower vendors, and product suppliers, and (3) marketing plan: what is your unique selling proposition — what sets you apart from others selling flowers? When I launched my yoga studio, Tranquil Space, in my living room in 1999, I set out with a small plan. I went through teacher training in June, began teaching at a local gym in August, and put up fliers in October inviting strangers to call me and reserve a spot for yoga class in my home. I believe it's best to leap: start small, grow organically, and see where the journey takes you. We'll explore being your own boss later in the book, but this gives you a taste of breaking down a one-year goal into actionable items.

Now, on to your five-year goals. These are the ones that may feel particularly far-fetched and scary, and it may take a while for you to see your progress. If you're feeling stagnant, remember that your dreams are still percolating within. It's like watching your hair grow: these long-term goals unfold slowly. Say a five-year goal is to have a cozy cabin in the woods far away from city life. Three action steps for making your cabin a reality may be: (1) save money: set aside 10 percent of your income and put it in a savings account specifically marked for your cabin, (2) do market

HAVE A PLAN

So, you want to launch a business? Similar to diving into your personal goals, writing a plan is a tool for pulling your business brainstorming together in a cohesive way. I've used my plans as guiding lights that ensure I stay on a forward-focused path. Here are the basic components of your plan:

1. Executive summary (mission, values, social responsibility, founder bio, location, overview of product/service, community involvement, legal structure)

2. Market summary (industry overview, target market, competitive analysis, SWOT analysis: strengths, weaknesses, opportunities, threats)

3. Marketing strategy (distribution of goods or service, public relations plan, sales strategy, product or service, strategic partnerships, promotions, trade shows, website, branding)

4. Management and operations (management team, organizational chart, distribution, fulfillment, research and development, technology, milestones, policies)

5. Financials (start-up costs, plan for funding growth, budget, cash flow projections, payroll, break-even analysis)

SAVVY SOURCE FOR FURTHER EXPLORATION

The Successful Business Plan: Secrets and Strategies, by Rhonda Abrams

Okay, darling, confession time: I created my first official business plan almost one year after I had started Tranquil Space. My motivation: I had to present it at graduation from my Women's Business Center course. Now I try to update it every few years to set new strategic goals and ensure I'm still on track with my original mission. My business plan serves as an ever-evolving road map.

research: begin looking online and in person for properties and locations, and (3) focus: start a wish list of what amenities and characteristics you want in your cabin — fireplace, two baths, A-frame, and so on.

The key with goals is to take the big picture and break it down into reasonable steps. Each week I keep a column in my planner titled "personal," and this is where I note action steps for my future goals. This guarantees that, during the day-to-day hustle, I am reminded of my big-picture goals. It is critical to stay aware of them amid the daily grind, otherwise you may come to a point in your life where you wonder what you've done with your time. Sound sadly familiar? Whatever you do with your list of action steps, make sure that it makes its way to a prominent spot, such as your closet, refrigerator, mirror, or planner. Keeping it tucked away in a journal may prevent you from receiving the continual tap on the shoulder it's meant to provide.

Take a Leap of Faith

One of my favorite yogis, David Swenson, teaches that there is good fear and bad fear. Good fear prevents us from stepping in front of a bus, while bad fear prevents us from taking risks. What's holding you back? For many, it is a fear of failure. For others, it is a fear of success. For some, it's sheer lack of will or knowledge of how to take risks. Remember what Eleanor Roosevelt said: "Do one thing every day that scares you." What will you do today?

RECURRING REFLECTION

As a devoted journaler, I find ongoing reflection to be an inherent part of who I am. It's important to downshift from overdrive to observe where you are, reward your efforts, and redirect yourself if you've turned off course. Following are a few ideas on implementing this sacred routine for reflection.

BIRTHDAYS. My "special day" is midyear, and this is a perfect time to do an assessment. A few years ago, I received an email from a friend wishing me a happy birthday and sharing an exercise she does annually. She encouraged me to make a list of everything I had accomplished since my last birthday and to make a list of everything I hoped to accomplish by my next birthday. Genius! Each year, I savor this exercise. It's rewarding to see what you've done in the past year while reviewing that list against what you had hoped to do. Plus, setting the stage for the following year by listing all you *will do* makes a fun kick-in-the-pants motivator.

CHANGE OF SEASONS. As nature changes around you (unless you live in, say, Florida), it prompts you to turn within and make your own changes. Each winter I grab a hot cocoa, curl up with a comforter, and pull out the Wheel of Life exercise, which you may have been exposed to during workshops, while working with a coach, or on any retreat with me. This exercise has you assess your level of satisfaction with areas such as health, home environment, education, finances, relationships, joy, creativity, self-care, career, and spirituality. Your level of satisfaction could easily change daily, depending on positive feedback at the office, a messy home, a breakup, or a lingering cold. By taking a look at these categories on a quarterly basis, you can establish action steps to move past stagnation. This also allows you to catch any brewing dissatisfaction that may be beneath the surface.

NEW YEAR'S. Reflection during this time of the year is a given. Most everyone creates some glorious resolutions that seem a distant memory by Valentine's Day. However, I encourage you to jump on this bandwagon too. Think of it as a science project. You may have recently done your seasonal reflections on or around the winter solstice, December 21, the darkest day of the year. New Year's is your chance to make sure you didn't miss anything on the solstice and to create action steps that will improve a sinking category in your Wheel of Life exercise. You have carte blanche to combine goals, reflection, vision boards (see the next section on vision boards), and action-step exercises as often as doing so keeps you moving ahead.

ANNIVERSARIES. These are special dates that signify something of importance to you. Maybe the death of a loved one, a wedding, a divorce, a big decision — whatever the occasion, take a step back on this date to reflect on a certain person, choice, or event. A celebration or a special ritual at your altar may even be appropriate. Take a moment to express gratitude for lessons learned or for time with this person, or think about what this day means to you overall and how this fits into your life.

RELIGIOUS HOLIDAYS. Some religions observe days (Yom Kippur, Christmas, Festival of Lights) or even months (Ramadan) of reflection. A friend of mine practices Shabbat from sundown on Friday to sundown on Saturday and doesn't work, get online, or spend money during that time, and instead enjoys simple pleasures and the company of friends. These sacred moments are a good time to slow down and become more introspective. It's like being given the green light for experiencing and enjoying the small things. Take full advantage of the holidays that speak to you, learn more about their meaning and significance, and feel free to dabble in some that are new. Doing so supplies a winning combo: you become more culturally literate and you turn within more frequently.

MORNINGS. As I noted earlier, taking the time to put pen to paper every day gives you a platform for ongoing reflection. This exercise can assist you in uncovering deep-seated dreams, hopes, and fears. Sometimes penning thoughts on the page can unleash ideas

33

that have been brewing deep within, searching for a way out. For example, I have used my journal to start lists of what I would need in order to launch a new business, or to write the ideal scene for my life in five years. When you are in that space where you're completely open, a whole new world can emerge. Given the chance, ideas will flow. Try this for a week: Keep your journal and pen next to your bed, and as soon as your satin eye pillow hits the nightstand, reach for them. Capture what comes up for you first thing in the morning.

VISION BOARDS

Creating a vision board is one of the most engaging exercises that I lead at retreats. Participants may come in as skeptics, but they always leave as believers with their vision boards proudly in hand. I receive photos from women around the globe sharing their vision boards, and I'm always awestruck when I see the images and quotes that are pulled together to make the unique final product. Vision boards are great for bringing one's dreams to life in a visually vibrant format.

In her book *Simple Abundance: A Daybook of Comfort and Joy*, Sarah Ban Breathnach speaks highly of vision boards and refers to them as "treasure maps." *The Secret*, by Rhonda Byrne, encourages the construction of vision boards as a way to bring what you want out of your subconscious through pictures and images. I've always called them collages, but I now prefer the glamorous term *vision board*. Whatever you call them, the intent is the same: capture your ideals, your dreams, your hopes on paper via magazine images, pictures, and words. Let this be a visual road map to fulfilling your dreams. Sound grandiose? Well, it is! I often receive follow-up emails from retreat participants raving about how this very exercise jump-started their lives and the changes they've made as a result. I can't speak more highly of this process for making things happen.

34

Design a Vision Board

Set aside two to four hours for this project. Turn off your phone. Light some candles. Turn up your favorite music. Surround yourself with a heap of your favorite magazines. Gather scissors, glue sticks, and glitter glue. Have file folders, construction paper, or scrapbooking paper handy for when you're ready to attach the images. Oh, and a trashcan for all your scraps.

Now that you have all your tools, begin flipping through magazines and tear out pictures and quotes that appeal to you. Find images that bring your vision to life based on your goals from the exercise on pages 27–28. Feel free to stop along the way to read an exposé that catches your eye. Let this time be playful and totally self-indulgent. You are, after all, creating your future. Might as well have some fun with it! Collect any photos, postcards, or notes from around your abode that might be inspirational to include. This hunting-and-gathering phase is the most time-consuming process of the project. But the results are well worth it.

35

Once you have a stack of images, begin cutting your favorites out of the torn pages. Place them on top of the thicker paper you've set aside as the backing. Arrange them in a way that looks pleasing, so that they become eye candy. You can group by category — style, home, garden, food, and so on — or have one big hodgepodge. If you're using a file folder as your backing, use the back and inside of it, too. If you're using a large sheet of card stock, don't forget the back. Sometimes we have too many images and too little space. Get creative. You can think (and glue) completely outside the board with this project.

Another option is to create a virtual design board. Pull images and quotes from the Internet, paste them into a document, and make it your screen saver. Use digital photos you've snapped along the way, images from Flickr, and online quotes that inspire you, and insert a photo of yourself into the fun. Or make this your desktop, and you can't help but be reminded of your vision every time you power up your MacBook. If you prefer the arts-and-crafts approach, but would like to use the image electronically, photograph or scan your masterpiece into a PDF or JPG file, and voilà, you can share the vision board on your blog, use it as a desktop, or pass it along to friends and family to help bring your ideas to life.

My latest vision board is full of style icons, pigs with pearls (I heart pigs), peonies in a vase, city terrariums, a *noir* French bulldog, a yogini in scorpion handstand, inspiring quotes, tips for decluttering, Ganesha looking over practicing yogis, iced sugar cookies and cupcakes (yum), a girl on a bike in the woods with a basket full of fruit, and rose petals. Basically, this is a feel-good vision board that touches on many aspects of my life: yoga, food, decor, fashion, nature, and inspiration — all things that I want to bring into my life or that I have that bring me happiness. There are numerous ways to do your vision board; just doing it is the point.

Images that align with your goals — such as a cabin in the woods, a woman holding a *bebé* while conducting a business deal, or a chic city loft — are important to have prominently displayed. Let them be regular reminders about what you are working toward. Indulge in an ornate frame for a smaller vision board or for displaying images of certain must-haves on your desk. What better way to keep yourself focused than through a beautiful reminder that you see daily? Now, wasn't that fun?

INTERNAL MUSINGS

Let's explore our own internal musings. Grab a cup of tea, pull out your journal, and let's take a moment to connect with your internal muse. Take ten deep breaths in through your nose and out the same way. Let the breath fill your ribs and chest. Reflect on the following questions and write out your responses.

1. Who do I admire as a muse?
2. What do I want to be my legacy?

3. If I did _____ in my lifetime, I would feel complete.
4. How do I want to make others feel when I address them in person, online, or through any other mode of communication?
5. What am I called to do?

BIRDS OF A FEATHER

We all know the adage "birds of a feather flock together." To achieve your aspirations, it is important to surround yourself with others who are also seeking to achieve their own. Some of my closest friends and I get together and regularly set or share goals over martinis some days, peppermint tea on others. Pull together a network of fabulous, well-intentioned, and supportive friends who can inspire you and help keep you on track. For example, if you're a recovering shopaholic, continuing to commune with your former shopping buddies on New York's Fifth Avenue would not be in your best interest. Rather, it would make more sense to seek out a new set of pals to mingle with at art galleries, at DIY classes, or while learning a new language. Associate with people who will lead (or at least copilot) you in the direction of your aspirations and inspire you along the way. Don't have any in your smartphone just yet? Join some like-minded groups and watch your social network grow. Trust me, it's good to choose your birds wisely.

37

ACT AS IF

Not quite feeling the aspiration love? Wondering how in the world you're going to open that business, raise a family, write that novel, or star on Broadway? Remember my ninth-grade "fake it 'til you make it" motto. You may be trembling in your stilettos, but never get up and declare, "I'm so nervous." Or you may be a brand new yoga teacher terrified to take a group of students through sun salutations. Again, don't fess up and say, "This is my first class, and I'm so nervous." That bewildered audience or class will be wondering why in the world you're up in front teaching them. The key is to just do it. Ask yourself, "What's the worst that could happen?" and put yourself out there. Everyone has to start somewhere. And everyone has a first time. Many people continue to be nervous after years of performing, writing, or public speaking. I'm not asking you to lie; I'm simply encouraging you to keep some things to yourself. Instead, get up there like you are the queen of Sheba: regal, deserving of attention, statuesque, and full of lots to say.

ASPIRATIONAL AFFAIRS

Throughout this section we've worked to get your aspirational affairs in order. You are full of dreams, and it's time to show the world what you've got to share. Take small steps each day to move in the direction of your aspirations. Keep them visible. Get a support network. Reflect regularly. And begin to act like the rock star you are.

MODEL MUSE

Thirty publishers rejected Sarah Ban Breathnach before she became the bestselling author of *Simple Abundance*. This beautiful book served up oodles of inspiration to me as I began my journey into adulthood after college. I've often touted it as the woman's bible — it's pink, chock-full of great tips on subjects ranging from style to home to food, and it feels like the BFF you wish you had. Sarah inspired me from an early age to set goals, keep persevering, and indulge in the simple comforts that bring great joy. In addition to being an inspiring author and speaker, she founded the Simple Abundance Charitable Fund and has donated over $1 million to more than a hundred non-profits. Learn more about Sarah at Simpleabundance.com.

3. DIVINE DO-GOODING

Never doubt that a small group of thoughtful, committed citizens can change the world. Indeed, it is the only thing that ever has.

— MARGARET MEAD

Doing good is no longer just for the bleeding hearts, but rather is a way of living. I love the notion of do-gooding and find it akin to breathing, bathing, and being. You cannot escape the continuous reminders to go green, be socially responsible, or save the planet. Our culture is infused with a sense of urgency to make a difference through our daily actions, decisions, and dollars. This section is full of ideas on how you can leave a lovely legacy not only by being you but also by reaching beyond yourself.

CHOOSE A CAUSE

There are so many worthy causes out there, and determining where to direct your efforts and energy is not always as easy as it sounds. You may be drawn to numerous issues and not sure how to narrow down the list. Taking the time to explore what moves you helps to ensure that you have the energy it takes to fight a potentially uphill battle.

What issue gets your riled up when you think about it? What cause would you spend your hours supporting if time or money were not concerns? Do you get teary over the polar bears' melting glaciers? Do you want to help hungry children in Niger? Is homelessness or domestic violence in your hometown a concern?

Does factory farming or the existence of puppy mills push your buttons? Take a moment to write out the issues close to you and note why they tug on your heartstrings. Now that you've honed in on your favorite cause or causes, let's explore ways to get out there and make a difference.

MAKE A DIFFERENCE

The options for doing something to support your cause and, at the same time, grow personally and professionally are endless. Following is a list of my favorite ways to get out there as a do-gooder and let your voice be heard.

Volunteer

Each month I head to a nearby assisted living center to offer up a dose of chair yoga to a variety of vibrant seniors. It's two hours a month out of my schedule to share basic breathing and stretching with an attentive and grateful audience. I always leave feeling better than when I went in. I chose this volunteer opportunity because teaching yoga is a skill of mine, and I've always been drawn to the delicate, loving nature of the elderly.

Think about your various skill sets, and explore ways that they may translate to your chosen cause or causes. Are you an avid event planner who could head a fund-raiser? Are you great with strategy and able to offer your business savvy to a fledgling nonprofit struggling to determine its mission?

Maybe it isn't so much a skill set as it is your lifestyle. Do you have a flexible schedule that allows you to walk dogs at the Humane Society during the day? Are you connected with lots of local celebrities and able to use your networking skills to help bring in a high-profile speaker? Think broadly and come up with innovative ways to support your favorite cause.

Of course, the donation of time in any capacity is good old-fashioned volunteering and can make a big difference to the organization. Organizations always need behind-the-scenes workers (administrators, organizers, letter writers) and frontline workers (for canvassing the streets, knocking on doors, making calls) to get things done. How can you volunteer in order to help the cause close to your heart?

Give Green

Set up an automatic-deduction giving plan. I have money automatically removed from a bank account monthly for a few special causes, and I donate to others as I can swing it. My businesses give a percentage of profits to diversified causes, plant a tree for every yoga class pass sold, massage given, and online order shipped, and have special events to benefit certain charities. Another way to donate is through one-offs such as natural disaster relief funds and presidential campaigns. Time may not be flowing in abundance for you, so you may prefer to donate money to your favorite cause.

41

Take a Volunteer Vacation

Wondering what to do with your next two weeks of vacation? Well, you can put your values to work by volunteering in a community in need. How about assisting with cleanup in an area after a natural disaster, teaching English, painting schools, or building and maintaining trails? Put your free time to work for a noble cause. Your spirit will thank you.

SAVVY SOURCES FOR FURTHER EXPLORATION

Globalvolunteers.org

Americanhiking.org

The 100 Best Volunteer Vacations to Enrich Your Life, by Pam Grout

Take Do-Gooding to Your Organization

Don't see many opportunities to reach out to the community and make a difference where you currently work? Well, why not ask your human resources folks if you can become the company's in-house karma director. Organize soup kitchen days, canned food drives, and clothing swaps, with leftovers donated to charity. Be the go-to person for people seeking ways to get involved in the community. Bonus: the organization will be touted as socially conscious, you'll emerge a leader, and you'll get to use your work time to serve others. Win-win!

Get on Board

Showcase your skills at an already-launched organization in need of leadership, decision making, and administrative work. Nonprofit boards are full of people passionate about a particular cause. Getting involved allows you to connect with like-minded leaders while assisting the growth of the organization. Seek out opportunities in your community. Send a letter to the organization's director outlining your passion, skill set, and experience that will translate into making you a strong board member. This is a big responsibility but also a critical step toward supporting your cause, enhancing your skill set, and becoming a thought leader.

Involve Your Friends

Social networking websites are an amazing (and easy) way to raise awareness. You can get donors and supporters and inform others about your passion in a few simple clicks. When gearing up for our nonprofit's annual gala, I invite many of my friends on Facebook to join the Tranquil Space Foundation page. All people have to do is click a box to join it, and then they are listed as supporters on their own profile page and on the cause's page. In addition, people can donate money easily through this page, and you can send announcements about events. Getting the word out these days is made so much easier through already-created networks such as Facebook.

Just Blog It

Want to inform others about your candidate of choice? Eager to start an online support group for parents of children with cancer?

Determined to save the dolphins? By using a free online blogging system, you can create an entire forum devoted to your cause. This can be a space for sharing resources, stories, volunteer opportunities, inspirations, and contact information for magazine and newspaper editors, congresspersons, and neighborhood commissioners, along with staggering statistics. The blogosphere serves as an accessible medium for letting your voice be heard while educating and inspiring others. (More techie how-to details later.)

Find Partners

Animal rights are close to my heart. When I decided to offer my first "doga" to raise awareness for one of our studio's main charities, the Washington Humane Society, I asked them to join me for the event. I also asked a local dog bakery to donate goodies for the pups. At doga events, I lead yoga, dogs run around with full bellies, and the Humane Society brings their adoption van — all for a requested donation of ten dollars to the cause. Partnering with the Humane Society allows us to do more than just send a check. They bring materials to hand out, people sign up for their mailing list and fill out applications for animal adoption, and the organization gains visibility by being in a local park on a sunny Saturday afternoon. The event has been going on for five years now and is a favorite among many local yogis and their beloved four-legged companions.

Can you find a similar synergy for your cause? Explore ways to align with other organizations, because it truly brings more bang for the energetic buck. By doing so, you'll gain more promotional outlets and a way for clients to learn about like-minded organizations, while creating *esprit de corps* for your special cause.

Mentor an Up-and-Comer

It's refreshing to work with an energetic, enthusiastic gal interested in learning more about your line of work or career path.

43

Taking time to share your expertise and nurture the mentee along her journey can produce great karma.

Reward Others' Good Deeds

Encourage others in your family, community, and organization to give back too. Give awards. Seek ways to acknowledge those who go above and beyond in do-gooding. Provide public kudos. Grant bonuses. Establish a special parking spot. Offer other special perks. At Tranquil Space we annually offer to pay teachers for five additional classes in exchange for twenty-five volunteer hours in the community.

Host a Drive

Collect canned food and help feed needy families in your area. Hold a toiletry drive to accumulate items for local shelters. Toy drives are thoughtful around the holidays. Gather coats, hats, and gloves during the colder months to help keep everyone warm. Target a specific need you see in your community — whether it is baby blankets or pet food. Provide a well-marked bin, and get the word out. This small gesture can reap amazing rewards. To make the exchange seamless, often the specific charity will pick up the items.

LAUNCH YOUR OWN NONPROFIT

Yes, this topic is a book in and of itself. Yet, having launched a nonprofit with a group of inspired individuals while sitting around my living room, I want to share my own experience and how-to in a nutshell. (Full disclosure: it helps that my beau happens to be a nonprofit attorney.) When I first began gathering industry information from local nonprofit directors, I had no idea what a 501(c)3 was. Acronyms and numbers that roll off the tongues of those in the nonprofit sector sound like a different language. Once you read *Nonprofits for Dummies* or speak to enough folks in the "industry," you no longer feel like such an outsider when you hear this lingo.

Building a business in a socially conscious way has been close to my heart since the humble beginnings of Tranquil Space in my fourth-floor walk-up. During a "sky is the limit" brainstorming session with a facilitator in the studio's early days, one of the ideas thrown out by a team member was a black tie gala for the studio's very own nonprofit. I giggled and thought the notion was too grandiose. Now, we host *annual* fund-raising galas for the Tranquil Space Foundation (only, they're not black tie — instead the dress is "cocktail chic").

One of my studio advisory board members mentioned the idea of funneling some of our donated dollars into our own cause, rather than distributing them all externally. I loved the notion of choosing a cause on which to focus our giving energy while also continuing to share resources with other organizations in a strategic way. The final push came, ironically, during a rock concert where the artist was showing images of children in Africa and raising awareness of the Clinton Foundation. It touched me, and I began to question how I could best use the studio as a platform for getting the word out about a cause. Who would have thought that a rock concert at Madison Square Garden would be such a catalyst?

The first step after chatting with local nonprofit in-the-knows was to find interested volunteers for the organization. We kept the volunteer board small to start, with *moi*, my nonprofit attorney beau, and a nonprofit guru who had been involved with the studio since class one in 1999. This allowed us to have impromptu midday meetings at cafés, come to consensus easily, and stay focused in our early stage. I printed a story about the opportunity to get involved in this nonprofit start-up in my yoga studio's monthly newsletter and was pleasantly surprised with the amount of interest I received from potential volunteers around the country.

During our first meeting we discussed the mission of the organization, and it took a few more sessions, and working with a consultant, to narrow down the cause. My interests ranged from the AIDS epidemic in Africa to animal rights to women's issues. Incorporating my master's in women's studies (with a focus on entrepreneurial leadership), and my passion for empowering women to think big and live fully, helped me narrow down the focus to females. After further exploration, we realized we wanted to offer tools to assist girls in the formative stage of their lives. Shortly after that we came up with the idea of bringing yoga, creativity, and leadership to girls in grades nine through twelve as our mission. All three of these topics are woven into a unique curriculum that helps bring a better sense of self to the girls we work with. Our hope is to expand this curriculum in the future to additional age groups across the country.

We worked with a local graphic designer to come up with a logo that was a spin-off of my yoga studio's logo to ensure consistent branding. My beau built our first website and filled out all the necessary IRS paperwork. I opened a bank account, and we tried (and tried...) to find a descriptive acronym to name our signature program (it seems like *all* nonprofits have pithy acronyms), but settled on Tranquil Teens: Stretch Yourself as the placeholder. Volunteers began forming the program's yoga, creativity, and leadership curriculum to fit a two-hour workshop format. We formed committees to help manage the larger steering committee (a group of volunteers not on the board): communications (marketing), programming (running programs and training Tranquil Teens facilitators), development (fund-raising), and generosity (giving away money to like-minded organizations).

With the realization that some volunteers come on board for only a few months before deciding they don't have the time, I determined we needed a better process, a list of expectations, and a coordinator of the volunteers. After showing up to facilitate programs at nonprofits with only one girl attending the event, we determined that the organization needed a coordinator of Tranquil Teens to serve as a liaison with the locations, to outline our expectations when bringing the program to their girls, and to be the go-to person for setting up programs. In addition, we created special committees for one-off fund-raiser events like planning our annual gala and hosting LUNAFEST. Setting up the infrastructure, outlining expectations, celebrating successes, emailing the minutes immediately after a meeting adjourns, and hosting two midyear review/goal-setting meetings has been critical to our growth as a volunteer-run organization.

Volunteer organizations and nonprofits with a laissez-faire attitude can leave those involved frustrated — because of last-minute calls or meetings, not starting or ending on time, not distributing minutes or meeting agendas, and overall disorganization. Starting a nonprofit is similar to starting a for-profit. It is critical to ensure efficiency and effectiveness in the setup and operations. The big awkward difference (for *moi*) is the constant requests for contributions. I tend to be a big fund-raiser for the Tranquil Space Foundation, but that is because I do it through my for-profit ventures. For example, I'll host a workshop or teleclass and give all the proceeds to the nonprofit. Or give a portion of sales from one of my other companies directly to the Tranquil Space Foundation. I'm not comfortable asking for money, and being able to do so is a skill critical to surviving in the nonprofit world. I'm just now getting used to that, but, again, it is critical to be able to tout the many reasons why your organization deserves others' hard-earned dollars and to be comfortable asking for them.

KEY FACTORS IN STARTING A NONPROFIT

1. CREATE YOUR CAUSE. Avoid duplicating. With over 1.5 million nonprofits in the United States, you must create something unique, or not yet in your region, or with a very

special spin. What gap needs to be filled? Crystallize your mission and determine your nonprofit's name.

2. SET UP A BOARD. Ideally one with a nonprofit attorney and accountant in tow. Keep it small and simple to start. Note the expertise you're seeking and review a list of friends or acquaintances to see the many skills already within your circle. Outline your expectations and the roles that need to be filled. Have expectations and role descriptions all spelled out in agreements to be signed by new board members. Set meetings well in advance to respect others' time, and pass along agendas in advance so that the board can come prepared. Reward your board often with gratitude and tokens of appreciation.

3. HANDLE NUTS AND BOLTS. Design a logo and website. Handle appropriate IRS paperwork and get directors' and officers' insurance. Set up a bank account and work with a nonprofit-minded accountant. I know, this is not the scintillating stuff, but it's the oh-so-important nitty-gritty that brands your organization and keeps you out of the pokey (always a good thing).

4. GATHER VOLUNTEERS. Do you need help with putting on special events, writing grant proposals, leading programs, handling email, reaching out to the community, or designing a website? Begin recruiting specialized helpers, and reach out to friends with a knack for the things you need. Be sure to outline your expectations, as you did when looking for board members. Put people in charge of certain committees or subcommittees — it engages volunteers to have something tangible to oversee. Reward often.

5. DO YOUR WORK. Get out there and let your voice be heard. Partner with local organizations. Host special events. Blog. Be a Facebook cause. Gather testimonials. Speak to the press. Attend aligned festivals and tradeshows. Get branded T-shirts for volunteers (and supporters) to wear. Be the change you wish to see, and help others to see your change.

THROW A CHARITEA SOIREE

All the ideas thrown at you so far may seem too involved or over-whelming, considering your available resources. A way to raise awareness (and funds or goods) for your favorite cause is by throwing a flair-filled fete. Who doesn't love parties? In my first book I touched on this concept and even created a downloadable tool kit to assist readers in bringing this idea to reality. Many good things start small and gain momentum through grassroots efforts. Good old-fashioned tea parties combined with activism can be a powerful and fun tool for change. A ChariTea soiree

SAVVY SOURCE FOR FURTHER EXPLORATION
Hiptranquilchick.com

helps build community and is a great networking experience. Invite five to fifteen people and ask each to bring like-minded friends. Perfect for getting your name out there as the do-gooding hostess with the mostess.

49

Here's the skinny: Hosting the soiree in your home allows you to create the complete vibe. If that isn't possible, look around for a cozy local café that has the same ambience you want to create. Following is the time line for pulling this off seamlessly and tranquilly.

Four Weeks Before

Determine charity to highlight, and request promotional materials.

Send invites to your fave gal pals and encourage them to bring two to three friends.

Invite a guest speaker from the charity.

One Week Before

Send reminder and directions.

Buy dry goods: drinks, treats, and candles, plus assorted

teacups, saucers, and cloth cocktail napkins from your local thrift store.

Purchase goody bags and their contents: a box of organic fair trade tea, organic fair trade chocolate, scented tea lights, bath treats, promotional materials from charity, tissue paper.

One or Two Days Before

Buy fresh food.

Create a playlist to set the mood (suggested: Madeleine Peyroux or John Coltrane).

Buy flowers.

Put together goody bags.

Day of Event

Tidy your surroundings.

Prepare food.

Set mood: light candles, arrange flowers, play the perfect music for your vibe.

Set up a treat and libation station.

Indulge in a restorative yoga pose prior to guests' arrival.

Don your most fabulous and comfy ensemble.

At Soiree

Be the hostess with the mostess: greet and introduce guests warmly, keep drinks and laughter flowing.

Introduce speaker from charity.

Day After Event

Send thank-you notes to guests, speakers, and helpers via snail mail.

TEA, TASTY TREAT, AND TRANQUILTINI MENU

Cucumber-mint and goat cheese–watercress tea sandwiches
Lemon cream scones
Cookies (butter and/or ginger are lovely tea accents)
Fresh fruit selection (assorted berries, green apples, pears)
Tea selection

Tea Brewing

An intoxicating brew of tea is essential. Begin with fresh, cold water, and heat it in a kettle on the stove. Prewarm the teapot by rinsing with hot water; a ceramic teapot provides the best heat and flavor. Measure one heaping teaspoon of loose-leaf tea per cup and add to the teapot. If using tea bags, count on one bag for each teacup. Remove the kettle from the heat when it has reached the just-boiling point, and pour immediately into the teapot. Cover the pot with a lid, and brew the tea for three to five minutes before pouring. The larger the tea leaves, the longer the brewing time. Remove the leaves or bags from the brewed tea to prevent bitterness. Serve with raw sugar, honey, or agave nectar.

Serve a variety of fair trade and organic green, white, and herbal teas, from chamomile to jasmine to chai. The Republic of Tea, Tulsi Tea, and Gypsy Tea have a plethora of tasty organic options.

Recipes for Treats

Cucumber-Mint Tea Sandwiches

These tea party favorites go perfectly with spearmint or peppermint tea.

½ cup loosely packed fresh mint leaves, finely chopped
4 tablespoons unsalted butter, softened
4 tablespoons cream cheese
12 slices of whole-wheat bread, crusts trimmed
6-inch length of seedless cucumber, cut into thin slices

In a small bowl, combine the mint, butter, and cream cheese, and stir the mixture well. Spread the bread slices with the butter mixture and top 6 of them with the cucumber. Distribute the cucumber evenly and season it with salt. Top the cucumber with the remaining bread slices. Cut each sandwich diagonally into quarters. Makes 24 tiny tea sandwiches.

Goat Cheese–Watercress Tea Sandwiches

These modern, savory tea sandwiches go well with green tea.

2 5-½-ounce logs of goat cheese, room temperature
½ cup chopped watercress leaves
16 thin slices of cinnamon-raisin, date, or other sweet nut bread, crusts trimmed
4 tablespoons unsalted butter, room temperature
1 cup finely chopped toasted pecans

Mix the goat cheese and chopped watercress and season with salt. Spread the mixture over 8 bread slices, then top with remaining bread. Butter edges of sandwiches. Cut sandwiches diagonally in half. Place pecans on a plate. Dip buttered edges of sandwiches into pecans. Arrange sandwiches on platter. Garnish with watercress sprigs. Makes 16 tea sandwiches.

Be creative with your tea sandwich breads. You can use wheat, pumpernickel, date-nut, and white breads, all with crusts trimmed and cut into small, triangular sandwiches. Plan on six to eight sandwiches per person.

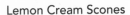

Lemon Cream Scones

These scones are the perfect accompaniment to floral and citrus teas.

2 cups all-purpose flour
¼ cup plus 2 tablespoons sugar
1 tablespoon baking powder
½ teaspoon salt
¾ cup chopped dried apricots (about 4½ ounces)
1 tablespoon plus 1 teaspoon grated lemon peel
1¼ cups whipping cream
3 tablespoons unsalted butter, melted

Preheat oven to 425°F. Mix flour, ¼ cup sugar, baking powder, and salt in large bowl. Stir in apricots and 1 tablespoon lemon peel. Add whipping cream and stir. Turn dough out onto lightly floured surface. Knead gently just until dough holds together. Form dough into a 10-inch-diameter, ½-inch-thick round. Cut into 12 wedges.

53

Transfer wedges to large baking sheet. Combine remaining 2 tablespoons sugar and 1 teaspoon lemon peel in small bowl. Brush scones with melted butter. Sprinkle with sugar mixture. Bake scones until light golden brown, about 15 minutes, then transfer to rack and cool slightly. Serve scones warm or at room temperature. Makes 12 scones.

TranquilTini

1 tablespoon lavender simple syrup (recipe follows)
2 ounces of vodka
3 to 4 ounces of sparkling water
3 to 4 ounces of pomegranate or cranberry juice

Combine the lavender syrup and the vodka in a cocktail shaker and shake with plenty of ice. Strain into an ice-filled highball glass, then top off with sparkling water and cranberry juice. Stir before drinking. Yum!

Lavender Simple Syrup

1 tablespoon dried lavender blossoms
½ cup sugar
1 cup water

Bring the lavender, sugar, and water to a boil in a small saucepan, until sugar dissolves. Simmer a few minutes and let cool before straining and storing in a glass or ceramic container.

Lavender Lemonade

8 lemons
11 cups water
1 cup dried lavender
1 cup honey

Remove zest from four lemons and squeeze the lemons for 1 cup juice. In a large pot, bring the water and the zest to a boil over high heat. Stir in the lavender. Partially cover the pot, lower the heat, and simmer for 10 minutes. While the water is simmering, place a large strainer lined with a damp paper towel over another pot. Strain lavender infusion. Press lavender to extract all liquid. Stir in honey until dissolved. Next add lemon juice. Let cool completely for approximately 45 minutes. Pour over ice and serve.

Serves 8.

Voilà, you have all the accoutrements for throwing a spectacular soiree with a socially conscious twist. Top off your event by hosting a clothing swap (all guests bring a few fave things from their closets that they are no longer wearing, and you all trade), and donate what is left to charity. Add in an additional activist speaker, such as a life coach, local musician, or indie designer, who will talk about making a difference through his or her work. Raffle off a session with this person or a piece of his or her work as an additional fund-raiser for your cause. The options for making your event a mindfully extravagant success are endless.

BE ECO-CHIC

Being green is no longer associated with envy: it's living a sustainable lifestyle, and its message is everywhere and in everything, from cars to makeup to clothing to investing, and it's imperative that we listen. Zero waste, recycling, and reusing were previously associated with being frugal; now it's admirable to be an ecominded frugalista. In the following list, I've pulled together a few of my favorite ways to be a savvy and budget-conscious do-gooder.

SAVVY SOURCE FOR FURTHER EXPLORATION
Boho Magazine: A New American Spirit

55

Reduce

Choose items with less packaging. Give gifts in reusable tote bags. Use cloth napkins over paper. Lessen your carbon footprint by choosing sustainable fabrics for clothing, decorating, and bedding. Ride your bike or walk. Plant trees to offset your carbon emissions. Choose locally grown produce. Avoid products from factory farms. Go vegetarian. Compost food scraps. Buy energy-efficient bulbs and appliances. Choose personal products not tested on animals. Find cleaning products made with plant- and mineral-based ingredients. Go on a necessities-only purchasing plan for a month — watch your wallet grow and your clutter decrease. Choose water-saver faucets, toilets, and showerheads. Take shorter showers. Rather than buying more stuff for family and friends during the holidays or birthdays, plant trees in their honor, give tickets to an exhibit, adopt rescue animals in their names, or give them memberships to a local theater or museum. Stop junk mail and catalogs. Get monthly financial statements online.

Reuse

I've always been a fan of secondhand shops, and now they're chic. My junior high pink-and-white-striped Jessica McClintock prom dress came from a secondhand store. Try your hand at shopping for fabulous finds at these beloved, economical stores. You'll find one-of-a-kinds and pay a portion of the price. By now, I know, you're toting your own reusable bag to the grocery store, but keep it handy for all other shopping opportunities, too. Done with that old tee? Turn it into leg warmers, arm warmers, a reusable tote, a tube top, or a cleaning cloth. Hang on to gift bags, maps, magazines, grocery bags, ribbons, and tissue paper for creative gift-wrapping. Choose reusable glass- and tableware when entertaining or packing a picnic. Pick up a reusable water bottle, such as one made by Sigg or Klean Kanteen — never be caught with a plastic water bottle. Buy used books. Swap books and magazines with others. Check out Freecycle.com. Becoming a do-it-yourself girl offers up the opportunity to shop stores such as Goodwill so that you can turn sheets into cosmetic bags, curtains into pillows, and clothing into handbags. Think "cheap chic."

Recycle

Check out rechargeable batteries. Switch to wind-powered electricity. Separate plastic, glass, and paper, and recycle it. Keep empty butter containers for storing leftovers. Keep empty pickle jars for storing paperclips or other small sundries. Clean remaining soy wax out of your glass candle containers and use them for nurturing cuts from your flourishing philodendron plant or storing Q-tips. Clean out your closet and donate what you no longer wear to charity.

SAVVY SOURCE FOR FURTHER EXPLORATION

The Eco Chick Guide to Life: How to Be Fabulously Green, by Starre Vartan

DO-GOODING DECIPHERED

Lots of ideas have been presented in this section, and this may have left your head spinning. You may wonder where to begin or how little ol' you can make a difference. Changing the world starts within, by changing yourself. Reflect on the cause close to your heart. Note the ways in which you can make this cause part of your everyday life. Throw a ChariTea soiree. Label yourself an activist. Observe your daily actions and determine ways to continue making them more green. Plant a tree. Be a mentor. Remember, be the change you wish to see.

MODEL MUSE

Rebecca Kousky founded Nest to support women artists and artisans in the developing world by helping them create sustainable entrepreneurial businesses. Tranquil Space Foundation chose this amazing organization to be a recipient of one of our own microgrants because Nest's support of women's creativity aligns perfectly with the foundation's values. As you know, throughout the centuries women have created not only utilitarian household objects and clothing for their families but also decorative objects. Rebecca emphasizes that entrepreneurial loans given to craftswomen let their arts become their livelihoods so that their decorative objects can be enjoyed by others. I proudly carry a tote from Nest's Guatemalan cooperative.

Rebecca's tagline is "Changing the world one purchase at a time," and she helps build nests for women around the globe. Rebecca, who has a master's in social work, launched Nest at the age of twenty-four and oversees an inspiring organization with offices in eight cities across the country. Shop her colorful website: Buildanest.com.

PART 2. BAKE IN BEAUTY

Our External Expression

4. CHIC CREATIVITY

There is a vitality, a life force, an energy, a quickening, that is translated through you into action, and because there is only one of you in all time, this expression is unique. And if you block it, it will never exist through any other medium and will be lost.

— MARTHA GRAHAM

The notion of creativity can be tricky to grasp. What exactly is it? Well, the art of being creative, of course. But what does "being creative" mean? Although I've read heaps of books and have focused on living creatively for the past decade, I still struggle to define the term. I first discovered that I was creative by reading books claiming that everyone is creative. Really, even *moi*? Although I've been addicted to accessories since my early years (picture a narrow pink belt worn over a black-and-gold first-grade soccer jersey topped off with a wide green headband), I never thought of myself as "creative" — a term reserved for painters or sculptors. You know, those who have their work on display and for sale. Since discovering that I, too, was a creative being, I've been on a crusade to inspire others to uncover their creative sides. This stage is all about unleashing your creative juices, exploring ways to live creatively, and basking in this state of expression.

YOUR LIFE IS ART

I like to think of each day as a fresh canvas full of possibility. Of course, there are days when you wake up and feel like nothing is in store, but stay with me. You can exude your creativity in numerous ways — from the clothes you wear to the color of the pens you use to the way you organize your files. Simple choices you make every day offer a welcome opportunity to think creatively. Begin to define your life as art — a true masterpiece. You already know you are one of a kind. Now revel in the creation of this magnum opus and consciously design your colorful canvas.

When you define your life as a work of art, each brushstroke, each decision, each person, each piece has significant value. Start to envision your life as the creation of a museumworthy masterpiece. What do you want to see — colors, players, life-defining moments, milestones? Let your canvas unfold in images that make your heart sing. You control your artistic touches and can start anew anytime. Every day, you are given a fresh canvas to paint with a renewed outlook. Enjoy the evolution of this ongoing work of art, and start to cultivate creativity in all you do.

ARTISTIC PLAYGROUND

Pull out some blank paper. Doodle. Add colors. Return to first-grade art class and color outside the lines. Consider whether your life as it is reflects the art that you want to share with the world. If not, remember that you hold the brush. Start painting!

INDULGE IN AN ARTIST DATE

Julia Cameron first exposed me to this little gem when I read her bestseller *The Artist's Way*. An artist date is a weekly two-hour solo excursion to indulge your creative side. I like to take this a step further with occasional solo nights, days, or even weeks. Think of your artist date as replenishing your creative well, nurturing your inner artist, and allowing yourself the chance to find inspiration. I've pulled together a plethora of options based on my own artist dates to offer ideas on indulging your creatress.

Bookstore Browsing

Nothing serves up happiness or inspiration quite like a big room packed full of books. My heart skips a beat when I step into a bookstore. Determining which section to hit first is the most anxiety-producing moment. Once I've decided, I settle into pure bliss. Bookstores offer ideas, creative thought, and tons of possibility. It's like going to a great movie and getting lost in another person's storyline for days. Now that many bookstores are equipped with cafés, the overall experience is even more sacred. Sip your favorite tea with a scone in hand, thumb through a stack of books, and have your journal nearby to capture inspirations. Ah, this is heaven on earth to me.

Art Galleries

Living in Washington, DC, definitely spoils me when it comes to fabulous art exhibits. I saw a jaw-dropping Edward Hopper exhibit and came home with a heap of postcards of his work and CDs filled with jazz music from the 1920s to the 1950s. As I do in bookstores, I find it delightful to see someone's creative expression in galleries — this time on canvas or sculpted in stone. When I first moved to the nation's capital, I used to hit the galleries and museums often, wandering the vast halls and bathing in the muses around me. Getting the chance to see paintings in person that you grew up seeing in textbooks — like Renoir's *Luncheon of the Boating Party* — is a religious experience.

You may not have access to large art galleries; if so, no matter. Take advantage of local art. Support aspiring friends' shows. Sip wine, mingle with like-minded folks, and take in the beauty of their creative expressions. Events such as these can help fuel your own creative spark. Or hop on a train to the largest nearby city and let the journey, plus the exhibit, be a full-fledged artist date. When I was eager to see the Pierre Bonnard exhibit at MOMA, I took a day off, bought my Amtrak ticket, and headed to New York. The day was magical, and I named my freshly found noir kitten Bonnard after this exhibit. Appreciating and reveling in other people's artistic expression can work its magic in wondrous ways.

Live Music

Going to see musicians play live is sure to jump-start your creativity. I've been to numerous Tori Amos shows solo over the years. Her music and performance persona always bring tears to my eyes. Seeing an artist in her element can leave even the most fledgling, aspiring performer feeling more connected to her own spirit.

Crafty Stores

Find a store full of fabric glue, watercolors, ribbons, rolls of fabric, and knitting needles, and you'll be in for a little slice of creativity heaven. Walking the aisles can fill your spirit with doses of color, texture, and ideas. Dabble in scrapbooking, stencil a blank tee, watercolor a postcard, or frame a print. Craft stores contain enough eye candy (and potential projects) to inspire your soul for years to come.

Dollar Stores

This may surprise you, but you can find lots of colored pencils, markers, construction paper, scrapbooking scissors, incense, scented candles, trinkets, stationery, gift bags, stickers, and notebooks for a fraction of the cost. Hitting these stores can be a fun way to stock up on inspiring tools and gifts for less than ten bucks.

Dance Performances

A dear friend has a belly dance studio, and I love going to watch the ladies perform in full stage makeup, including glitter and long feathery eyelashes, along with extravagant costuming and tons of accents in their hair. I find myself dancing to the beats in my seat and daydreaming about joining a touring troupe.

Nature Expedition

Why not spend your lunch hour on a nearby patch of grass, or take a Sunday drive to your state park? Have your sketchpad and journal in tow to capture inspiration as it arises. Communing with nature assists with getting your spiritual connection on. Have you found the nearby arboretum or botanical gardens? Listen to birds, watch the squirrels, and gaze at the stars. Nature encourages you to slow down and relish magnificent vistas — and often you can do this without having to travel too far.

Matinee Mojo

65

I'm a sucker for matinees on weekdays. Ever since I saw my first flick solo, I've been hooked. Going to movies alone is oddly empowering. Movies are creative genius given life on a big screen. Taking an afternoon to partake in someone else's reality can help relax you and clear your head — kind of like hitting a reset button. This may not seem terribly productive, but I promise you that downtime opens up your creative channels in miraculous ways.

DIY DIVA

Getting crafty has become incredibly chic. There are books, classes, centers, and even a TV station devoted to helping you get your craft on. Following are a few of my favorite ways to indulge my DIY side.

BEAD A NECKLACE. Choose your beads and gather your supplies. You'll need two crimps, wire, a design board, a closure,

SAVVY SOURCE FOR FURTHER EXPLORATION

Get Your Sparkle On: Create and Wear the Gems That Make You Shine, by Lindsay Cain and Sarah B. Weir

flat-nose pliers, and scissors. Lay your beads out on the board in a design that most appeals to you. Thread the wire through the beads and leave a few extra inches. Add the crimp to one side and then the closure. Slide the wire back through the crimp and use your flat-nose pliers to close it tightly. Clip off excess wire. Repeat on the other side.

MAKE ARM WARMERS. Find an old sweater and collect your scissors, a seam ripper, straight pins, a sewing machine or needle, and thread. Cut off the sweater sleeve about three-quarters of the way up the arm — this will leave it long enough to cover your arm from knuckles to elbow. Use as a guide for the second sleeve. Turn one sleeve inside out, and use your straight pins to make the sleeve fit snugly around your wrist area. Sew the pinned area. Trim off excess fabric. Hem the cut edge by folding it over one-half inch and sewing it (still inside out). Use a seam ripper to open up a thumb hole two inches from the bottom. For additional support, stitch around the thumb hole.

TURN YOUR LONG-SLEEVE TEE INTO A BUBBLE TUBE. Collect some elastic, your sewing machine, straight pins, needle, and thread. Turn your tee upside down and inside out. Remove all the hem stitching and open up the hem. Place elastic along the old hem crease (measure above your boobs to get the right tightness in the elastic), stitch or safety-pin the ends of the elastic together, fold the hem over the elastic, and sew the hem down. Turn it right side out, slip it on, and tie the long sleeves in front or back like a sash. If you need to widen the neckline-turned-bubble-hem, open it up slightly by cutting around the original opening. Voilà, you have a uniquely yours bubble tube top.

SAVVY SOURCE FOR FURTHER EXPLORATION

99 Ways to Cut, Sew, Trim, and Tie Your T-Shirt into Something Special, by Faith Blakeney, Justina Blakeney, Anka Livakovic, and Ellen Schultz

MODES OF CREATIVITY

You may be wondering how seeing your life as art and partaking in artist dates applies to you, especially if you aren't sure where your creative flair lies. That's what we'll explore in this next section. I've gathered an assortment of ideas to help you as you use twelve fabulous methods to dabble in creative expression. Some of these mediums have submediums, so just remember, there are thousands of ways for you to express your creativity, and in this stage we're just skimming the surface while introducing you to some favorites.

Writing

So you think you have a novel inside you? Maybe a screenplay or memoir? Or simply a good, old-fashioned how-to article? Well, getting it out is an ubercreative process, and seeing your words come to life on a page or stage or in a movie theater can be absolutely thrilling. Not sure where to start? By capturing your thoughts, of course. Sounds easier than it is, trust me. The key is to start writing now. Pull out a kitchen timer, set it for ten minutes, and begin writing on your laptop or pad of paper. Commit to writing ten minutes each day for a week, and watch an epic unfold. Sign up for a writing class, or launch a writing group with a few of your closest girlfriends. Assignments and set meeting times will help you stay on track, and your classmates or friends will offer camaraderie and feedback.

Writing a blog is another fun way to get started. It offers instant gratification because, with the click of a button — voilà — you're published for the entire world to see. No pressure, eh? Blogs offer you a chance to receive feedback from your audience, and this will give you the opportunity to see if you're on the right track. Many larger projects have been launched through this humble means.

How about writing an article and pitching it to a magazine?

SAVVY SOURCE FOR
FURTHER EXPLORATION
Writing Down the Bones,
by Natalie Goldberg

I started with small niche newsletters, local newspapers, and alumnae magazines, which are hungry for material and have smaller budgets. Seeing your name in print can be rewarding, and it serves as inspiration to keep writing. The world wants to hear what you have to say. Promise.

Music

Interested in learning to play the guitar, drums, or piano? What about singing or songwriting? I promise there is a means for you to learn — book, tutor, DVD, CD, group classes, or other. The options are endless. Let your inner rock star come out for a visit. You may just surprise yourself.

Dancing

As a young girl I danced in order to perform in annual recitals. Nothing beats getting all made up, dressing to the nines in sparkles, and heading on stage to strut your stuff after rehearsing for months. As an adult, you can still experience this glamour, but your parents may not be in the audience recording like they were when you were five. Wanting to reconnect with my inner ballerina, I took a ballet class with heaps of other uncoordinated adults a few years ago, and was incredibly humbled. As I scuffled like a crab (rather than sashaying) across the floor, I realized that my time as a balle-

SAVVY SOURCE FOR
FURTHER EXPLORATION
Masters of Movement:
Portraits of America's Great
Choreographers,
by Rose Eichenbaum

rina had come and gone. Despite that realization, I continued to show up for class and hold my head high. Inspired, I've also taken swing, salsa, and hip-hop classes. It's so fun to get your body moving and learn new things. Why not sign up for tango or ballroom dance classes? You may not give the performance of a lifetime, but you'll have a few good belly laughs trying!

Art

I use this term generically to cover a few mediums, such as pottery making, sculpting, drawing, and painting. This is what many people think of when they hear the word *artist*. Trying out things you've picked up from a book, taking a group class, or working one-on-one with a tutor offers you a chance to create in ways you may have never thought possible. There is something incredibly sexy about working with clay, or taking your palette, easel, and canvas to the local park to capture fall foliage. And if you don't discover that you're the next Georgia O'Keeffe, it's okay. Enjoy the process and honor yourself for stepping outside your creative comfort zone.

Photography

In this delightful age of digital photography, it's amazing how easy it is to capture a moment. Begin carrying your digital or Flip camera around and snap images that catch your attention. I have tiny ones that I keep in my purse (along with the connector cable) to capture people, places, interesting displays, flowers, my dog, fashion, products — anything that makes me smile or brings inspiration in the moment. You can post the images on your blog, YouTube, or Facebook or showcase a collection to display at a local café. I grew up with a darkroom in my home, thanks to a father passionate about capturing images in the predigital days. Bringing a moment or object to life with the right frame and the right eye can move people. We've all been affected by photos that touched us; now it is your chance to capture images that tell your story and that can have an effect on another.

Fashion

Ooh la la, one of my favorite topics, and we have a whole upcoming section dedicated to overall style. This is an easy way to express creativity, since you have to get dressed every day. Change the way you think about this — you're not just getting dressed for work, you're showcasing your style! Take a sewing class; this

SAVVY SOURCE FOR FURTHER EXPLORATION

Born-Again Vintage: 25 Ways to Deconstruct, Reinvent, and Recycle Your Wardrobe, by Bridgett Artise and Jen Karetnick

experience is truly empowering. There are so many amazing pieces that you can make with basic sewing skills. My mum could whip up a new wardrobe in a matter of hours, and I *was* the Home Economics Queen in ninth grade (never mind my finger's run-in with the sewing machine). I feel like sewing is in my blood — although my skill set may show the contrary.

Even if sitting down to a sewing machine feels impossible, there's a ton you can do with fabric glue and a needle and thread. Pick up one of those amazing books that gives you over a hundred options for clothing, accessory, and home decor items that you can make with a T-shirt. Try your hand at tie-dyeing. Go crazy with appliqués. Cut up an old sweater or blanket and turn it into leg warmers.

Food

While I'm partial to organic frozen food, I do appreciate a tasty home-cooked meal. Plus, I know many people find this process to be incredibly creative. Not sure if cooking is for you? Try a cooking class, or trade a bottle of wine with a foodie friend for a lesson in some of the basics. Pick out a yummy but simple-sounding recipe, gather the ingredients, and whip up something special. Just be sure not to mistake powdered sugar for flour. I did this once and my mother has never let me forget it. (White powdery substances look alike....) Cooking blogs, cookbooks, TV shows, and columns are uberpopular and available for foodies. Resources abound.

If you're interested in hosting a dinner party, don't think you have to make everything from scratch. Entertaining can be a creative endeavor. Your only recipe may involve pouring the bag of precut lettuce into a big bowl and adding tomatoes, mandarin oranges, green apple slices, and candied pecans. Everything else may be frozen hors d'oeuvres that you serve as tapas, topped off with cupcakes from your local bakery for dessert. Sometimes the creativity lies in the setup for eating, rather than the food itself. Fold cloth napkins into doves, design a beautiful centerpiece with votives and flowers, and make your plates of food artistic presentations with sprigs of rosemary, pomegranate seeds, or chocolate sauce dribbled on your dessert plate. Even if you usually use your kitchen as additional closet space, let yourself shine by throwing a beautiful dinner party.

SAVVY SOURCE FOR FURTHER EXPLORATION
The Last-Minute Party Girl: Fashionable, Fearless, and Foolishly Simple Entertaining, by Erika Lenkert

71

Crafting

Knitting has become superchic over the past decade, with stores devoted to the craft popping up in big cities. Crocheting uses one less needle and is also a popular craft — perfect for making blankets for all those darling newborns in your circle. Beading is a playful excursion from daily to-dos. It's amazing to see how quickly you can have your own one-of-a-kind jewelry collection for a fraction of the cost. With a few simple tools, some sparkly beads and other findings, you can make all sorts of fancy necklaces, earrings, and bracelets. Scrapbooking falls into this category and is such a popular pastime that you can find all the necessary accoutrements at your local dollar store. Stamping is also fun and addictive. There are stamp colors and stamp designs galore. You can even have custom stamps created with your logo, name, or a special

SAVVY SOURCE FOR FURTHER EXPLORATION
The Big-Ass Book of Crafts, by Mark Montano and Auxy Espinoza

image. Perfect for adding a touch of flair to your snail-mail notes, gift bags, invitations, or letterhead.

Decorating

Collecting swatches, paint chips, and images from decor magazines is a fun if slightly overwhelming project when working to define (or redefine) the look of a space. The devil is in the details, and overseeing a decorating project is exciting, but it can also be decision overload. From paint color to flooring to fixtures to prints to lighting — the list goes on and on. If this creative endeavor is new to you, start small

SAVVY SOURCE FOR FURTHER EXPLORATION
ReMAKE ReSTYLE ReUSE: Easy Ways to Transform Everyday Basics into Inspired Design, by Sonia Lucano

with a bathroom, closet, or nook. Choose your style — bohemian, classic, eclectic, cottage — and let the look evolve over time. Let your career as a decorator begin with some new soy candles, fresh flowers, or updated photo frames. It doesn't have to be a huge overhaul. The key is to keep the process fun, fresh, and innovative.

72

Gardening

The act of planting something and watching it grow can be rewarding. We, too, are little seedlings constantly growing, thanks to water, love, and light. Plant a few herbs in pots on your apartment windowsill or an entire wildflower garden in your backyard to get a little glimpse of Central Park in your own 'hood. This endeavor takes a few gardening tools, soil, seeds or seedlings, sunlight, and a dash of know-how.

SAVVY SOURCE FOR FURTHER EXPLORATION
You Grow Girl: The Groundbreaking Guide to Gardening, by Gayla Trail

Acting

I have friends obsessed with improv and have gone to see others perform in rousing local plays. I hear only rave reviews from people who take classes in said subject. Why not audition for your local theater's upcoming performance? When I go to see plays, I'm always impressed with the laundry list of performances under the actors' bios. I was once an apple in our church's rendition of Shel Silverstein's *The Giving Tree*. You have to start somewhere, and yes, your small community play counts. If this is a dream of yours, begin to explore the possibilities and you may find a hidden talent.

SAVVY SOURCE FOR FURTHER EXPLORATION

The Creative Entrepreneur: A DIY Visual Guidebook for Making Business Ideas Real, by Lisa Sonora Beam

Building a Business

Launching a business is one of the most innovative and challenging ways to express your creativity. Choosing a logo, color scheme, tagline, and way of offering your product or service; naming the organization; and designing a website are all creative decisions to be made by the creatress in charge. More on this seductive topic in sections 6 to 8.

73

WAYS TO EVOKE CREATIVITY

Forcing creativity is akin to bathing a cat. The key is to be deliberate about it. Set the stage to let it flow. While working to meet deadlines in the face of writer's block, or to juggle multiple creative sparks, I have found that four tools are critical to my creative success. Following are my life-saving creative tools.

Have a Ritual

When I sit down to indulge in a creative endeavor, I often light a candle. It's important to turn off the influx of email, set my cell phone on silent and put it way across the room, clear my work space of clutter, have a cup of tea nearby, and play ambient music in the background (unless I'm writing — then I need pure, blissful silence). I also find it critical to be dressed in something comfy that feels well put together — accessories, lip gloss, and all. But that's me; it's important to explore what works for you.

How can you make your creative time sacred? Try taking a hot bath before sculpting. Painting your nails before writing. Baking bread before gardening. Spending time at your altar before dancing. Meditating before sewing. Whatever it is, turn it into a regular ceremony that prepares your mind, body, and spirit for creative expression.

Set Up Your Space

We all know Virginia Woolf strongly suggested that women have a room of their own. I believe it is necessary, whether you are creating or not. But for artistic play, it is critical that you have a special space to store your tools, display your design boards, feel safe, come for inspiration, and file your ideas.

74

Design boards are the perfect place to post swatches, images, cards from fans, color chips, and artistic postcards so that you'll have inspiration at your fingertips. Ensure that your space is well stocked with pens, paper, and creative tools such as needles, paintbrushes, or wire. Lighting can assist with creating ambience, but in your workspace it is critical to have lots of lighting to prevent your having to squint — remember, darling, squinting promotes wrinkles.

SAVVY SOURCE FOR FURTHER EXPLORATION

Where Women Create: Inspiring Work Spaces of Extraordinary Women, by Jo Packham

Manage Your Time

Carve out space for the creativity to flow, and have patience if it doesn't flow as quickly as you'd like. A kitchen timer can be a handy tool for all sorts of discipline: meditation, creating, yin yoga, and taking small chunks of time to focus on a bigger goal. If you are heavily scheduled (aren't we all?), it's key to use the space between obligations for making things happen. Rushing from one meeting, class, or call to the next can leave you twiddling your thumbs between appointments, since there isn't enough time to launch into another project. Take advantage of the in-between time to open your Word document and add fifteen minutes' worth of writing to your novel. Sometimes you have to steal what little in-between time you have. Have your journal or idea book handy at all times for brainstorming and for capturing fleeting ideas.

I try to allocate one day a week for creative flow. During this time I muse on new designs for my ecoclothing line, TranquiliT, write, bead chunky gemstone necklaces, organize my living and work space, take hot baths, and daydream. This creative space is critical to refueling my often depleted well. Review your schedule right now and observe where you can carve out at least fifteen minutes weekly to work on a creative project. This is *in addition* to the weekly artist date. I know, I never said the journey to enlightened work and mindful play was easy. But creativity is critical for your soul's survival, so do all you can to make it happen.

Return to Yoga

When leading yoga and creativity workshops, I love to bring in the tenets of yoga and share how they apply to our creative process. *Tapas* means "discipline." To create you must be strict about sitting down or getting out there and making it happen. *Ahimsa* is nonviolence and is critical to the creative process. Of course your first draft or performance won't be your strongest, but you must practice kindness toward yourself on the creative journey. Self-study, *svadyaya*, ensures the continued connection of your spirit to your creativity. By reflecting regularly, you are able to grow, improve, flourish, and change course, as needed. *Santosha* is the practice of being content with what is. So your book signing drew a small crowd — it drew a crowd (even if it was your family), and that is what you must focus on to stay inspired. *Saucha* means "purity" and brings us back to the

SAVVY SOURCE FOR FURTHER EXPLORATION

Hip Tranquil Chick: A Guide to Yoga On and Off the Mat, by Kimberly Wilson

importance of setting up an organized creative space and keeping our insides pure by consuming healthy food and drink and getting exercise. All these practices will assist the creative flow.

LET YOUR LIFE SPARKLE

Creative expression is a right, and a necessity for your continued exploration of yourself, especially while you're on a more mindful path. Explore ways to add more color, glitter, laughs, and light to your everyday. Put your personal stamp on everything that you put out in the world. You are unique, no doubt about it. Let your authentic spirit shine forth and sparkle brilliantly.

MODEL MUSE

The lovely Midwestern designer Amy Butler oozes creativity — from her books to her sewing patterns to her stationery to her organic bedding. She has taken her creative passion and grown it into an inspiring business that helps fuel other women's creativity. I've used her ornate paper for crafts, tried designs from her book *In Stitches*, and thoroughly enjoyed my interview with this down-to-earth designing diva. Amy exudes Midwest charm, humility, and a balanced work ethos and is sure to light a creative spark and have you wishing she was your BFF. What began with twelve hundred dollars has turned into an empire of creative expression. Learn more about Amy at Amybutlerdesign.com.

5. SUSTAINABLE STYLE

Fashion is not something that exists in dresses only.
Fashion is in the sky, in the street, fashion has to do
with ideas, the way we live, what is happening.

— COCO CHANEL

You've seen her. The girl who embodies style. Head-to-toe co-ordination. The perfect outfit. Matching accessories. Head held high. Pearly smile. Graceful gestures. Hair perfectly coiffed. Belle of the ball.

The Greek philosopher Epictetus said, "Know, first, who you are; and then adorn yourself accordingly." We've spent the past few sections exploring who we are, and now we get to play. That's what this section is all about — adorning your body (*corps*), your home (*maison*), and your life (*vie*) with your special touch. Style is an outward reflection of what is within. We'll begin our exploration of sustainable style on a personal level, and then take it into home and overall self-care.

LE CORPS

Do you go to a conservative or creative office? Do you work from home? Do you have a uniform? Answers to these questions de-termine what you put on every morning. When we get dressed each day, we have a chance to express our signature style. There is always room for creative expression through your clothing, even if you must don a less-than-sassy khaki uniform. We'll explore the fundamentals for building a versatile wardrobe and accessories that can add panache to your basics.

As a designer of ecofashion, I love to talk clothing — especially chic and comfy togs. When I launched the TranquiliT line in 2002, it consisted of printed T-shirts and capri and drawstring yoga pants. I wanted a flattering line that I could live, work, and play in. TranquiliT has evolved over the years into a true lifestyle line that can be worn to yoga classes, weddings, the beach, art exhibits, even inaugural balls. Girls-on-the-go need versatile pieces that simplify their everyday dressing dilemma. You have enough drama to fret over; why make getting dressed part of it? Following are suggestions for infusing your wardrobe with a dose of eco-extravagance.

Top Workday-to-Everyday Staples

In this era of simplicity, let's pare down to the basics and use pieces that transition from workday to evening and beyond. When possible, seek out local designers and sustainable fabrics, such as organic bamboo, hemp jersey, and organic cotton, or hit the racks of your local secondhand shop. Here's a list of my favorite must-haves for exuding signature style from work to play.

PALAZZO PANTS. Perfect for the office, the beach, and wearing over your fitted workout bottoms.

LITTLE BLACK DRESS. A must in every modern girl's closet. Also great for travel in a wrinkle-free fabric. Pull your hair up and don faux pearls and kitten heels at the office. Let your hair down and don a layered chain necklace and strappy metallic sandals for a night out.

FITTED TEES. Everyone needs a basic, flattering black tee and white tee. And if you enjoy splashes of color, here is a great place to add them.

LONG-SLEEVE WRAP OR CARDIGAN. Great for throwing on in over-air-conditioned offices or airplanes, and it serves as a nice cover-up over your fitted tee. A vintage broach adds decorative flair for holding it in place.

ALL-IN-ONE WRAP DRESS. Wear as a one-shoulder dress, a long skirt over your swimsuit, or a tube dress for a summer soiree. This piece is the ultimate in versatility.

SAVVY SOURCE FOR FURTHER EXPLORATION
TranquiliT.com

DARK ORGANIC COTTON JEANS. Darker jeans are dressier, so you'll get more use out of this sassy shade.

BLACK SUIT WITH PENCIL SKIRT. Even if you left corporate America long ago, a classic suit in your closet will serve you well. Channel Coco. You might not wear the pieces together, but you'll have a timeless blazer to throw over dark jeans or your black pants, and a pencil skirt to top off with a fitted cardigan. Great for your "making an impression" gigs.

LONG, FLOWY SKIRT. Ideally, choose one with a waistband that allows you to pull it up over your chest and use it as a tube dress. I heart versatility!

LIGHTWEIGHT SHAWL. Throw it over your shoulders, use it as a lap blanket, wrap it around your hips at the beach, or channel Jackie O by wearing it as a head wrap with big sunglasses.

DUSTER. A loose, lightweight knit jersey or sweater for those chilly mornings. Add a flower pin for a cheerful effect.

When determining your wardrobe, think ease. Focus on mixing and matching various pieces. This will make packing for your next getaway, and everyday dressing, feel like you're creating a work of art.

PERFECTLY CHIC ENSEMBLES
FOR EVERYDAY OCCASIONS

POOLSIDE: Bikini, lightweight shawl, good book, big sunglasses, and straw hat.

THEATER: Little black dress, long faux pearls, arm warmers, and patent clutch.

YOGA: Leggings; long, fitted tee that covers your bum; and long-sleeve wrap for final relaxation.

DANCING: Palazzo pants, fitted tee, and long-sleeve wrap top, tied in front ballerina-style.

AT THE EASEL: Dark denim jeans, duster, and beret with sparkly broach.

80

WEDDING: All-in-one wrap dress worn as a one-shoulder.

JET-SETTING: Palazzo pants, fitted tee, duster, and shawl.

MEDITATION: Leggings, fitted tee, and shawl to keep your shoulders or lap toasty.

LOUNGING: Palazzo pants, fitted tee, long-sleeve wrap top, and headband.

SAVVY SOURCE FOR FURTHER EXPLORATION

A Year in High Heels: The Girl's Guide to Everything from Jane Austen to the A-list, by Camilla Morton

WINE TASTING: Long skirt, fitted tee, and shawl to double as a makeshift picnic blanket.

OFFICE: Black pencil skirt, fitted tee, and ecocashmere cardigan.

PREGGERS: Leggings or palazzo pants, and all-in-one wrap dress as a top.

SPEAKING ENGAGEMENT: Suit jacket, palazzo pant, and fitted tee.

Accessories: Touches to Make Your Style Shine

I heart accessories. The more, the merrier. Coco Chanel reminded women to always remove one of their accessories before leaving the house. Less is more, she believed. It's a personal choice. Are you bohemian or classic? Bold or more conservative? To assist with pulling together a toy box of playful trimmings, I have concocted a list of my faves:

ARM WARMERS. Sweater, velvet, or stretch jersey for yoga, dancing, or balls.

HEADBANDS. Wide, thin, double-strap, and with flowers attached, all help with flyaway hair.

LEG WARMERS. Keep your calves toasty with sweater leg-warmers or shiny over-the-knee socks.

EARRINGS. Dangly, studs, peacock feathers, and lightweight shells make your face sparkle.

NECKLACES. Long beads, chains, and chokers, used in layers add the perfect accent.

BRACELETS. Bangles, mala meditation beads, and gemstones add color or texture to your ensemble.

SCARVES. Throw over your shoulders, tie in your hair, wrap around your neck or around your head à la Audrey, or tie around your wrist for a very feminine or mysterious look.

SHOES. Ballet flats, tall boots, stilettos, kitten heels, ankle boots, Wellies, sling-backs, flip-flops (a must for your pedis), sneakers (only if you run), and wedges finish off your look in style.

EYEGLASSES. The four-eyes look equals intellectual. Embrace it and flaunt it. Sunglass in style.

OUTERWEAR. Trench, duster, and faux fur (straight from Grandma's closet).

BAGS. Patent clutch, bon voyage luggage, basic overnighter, and everyday (love my Anna Corinna) to haul your journal, credit cards, and lipstick.

BELTS. Wide with fancy buckle or narrow and barely there to cinch your drapey top.

MAKEUP MUST-HAVES

Adorning your face with color is a personal expression of style. The options are overwhelming, and the fundamentals are few. Weed out your cosmetics regularly, especially those you tote around daily. I find that my pink leopard-print makeup bag gets heavier by the week, so I have to "spring clean" it often.

Here are the basics that I recommend all ladies have on hand: slanted tweezers to keep your brow arch in line; lip gloss to keep your pucker soft, shiny, and colorful; a tinted moisturizer with sunscreen to smooth your complexion while keeping the sun's rays at bay; a powder to control shine; and mascara to frame the windows to your soul. Additional items of flair include eyeliner (love the black cat-eye look — très French), lip liner to blend with clear gloss, and sparkly faux eyelashes (fun for the holidays or a weekday soiree).

Hair

Ah, your crowning jewel. Your locks have a lot to say about who you are. Do you spend hours styling your tresses in the morning or rush out the door with them still damp? Are you an every-six-weeker at the salon, or do you go just when you can't take the frizzy, split-end look another day? Do you wear it up or let it flow freely? The key to stylish hair is ease. Be playful. Try a new color or hint of a new color (low lights or highlights). Play with a henna over-the-counter semipermanent color. Let your mane be a trademark for your style. Your eating and drinking (and — gasp — smoking) habits all show up in your hair. When you take good care of your innards, your locks will reflect their appreciation.

Your hair deserves oodles of TLC, considering all it is put through — pulling, straightening, blow-drying, curling, coloring, bleaching. It's surprising that I have any hair left, after all I've put it through over the years. However, I am religious about my trims every six weeks, and I now let the natural oils seep in by washing only a couple times per week. When you wear your hair curly or pinned up, the oils aren't as obvious. The key to good hair care is to work with what your parents gave you. Sure you can add a splash of color here and there, but it's critical to nourish your hair. Here are a few tricks:

- To make your own deep conditioner, whip up one cup of avocado paste with the yolks of two eggs. Apply for half an hour and then wash it off with lukewarm water.

- Use gentle organic hair products and avoid sodium lauryl sulfate, which is found in many shampoos — it's uberdrying. Boo.

- Avoid pulling your hair back with tight bands, as it promotes breakage and headaches. Instead use a clip with teeth. Twist curly hair into a funky bun, and use a few clips for a festive look.

- Cut down on washes. This saves money on product and lets your natural oils prevent dehydration of your scalp and hair.

83

- Indulge in a deep conditioning at least quarterly. Use the recipe I've given at the start of this list, or your salon will be able to indulge you, as will your local drugstore.
- If you're a highlight queen like *moi*, go for a partial highlight rather than full. Saves money and time, and let's be honest, who cares what color your hair is underneath?

FANCY UP YOUR EVERYDAY "DO"

- Wear it in a bun and flaunt your inner ballerina.
- Twist your hair into small sections and use bobby pins or small clips to secure the sections into place. This creates a funky, artistic hair display and is great for those in-between-haircut, -color, or -wash days.
- Don a headband or sparkly hairpins.
- When your hair is still wet, keep your curl by adding a moisturizing curling cream, dividing your hair into two ponytails, scrunching them into two funky buns, and clipping them above your ears. When you remove the clips a few hours later, your curls will be picture perfect. Ooh la la!
- Go to the salon for a blowout. Better yet, set aside twenty to thirty minutes and do it yourself at home.
- Try two side ponytails or braids. Schoolgirl chic and perfect for your yoga shoulderstand.

Mani/Pedi

As a yoga teacher, I've found monthly pedicures to be critical to my profession. Just recently I've begun to dabble in biweekly manis and have developed a penchant for *très* dark shades. These small touches add nice color to my everyday. I feel more feminine with painted nails and love that I can accessorize my hands.

Thank goodness there are now many "green" polish options out there. Do your research and bring your own polish to the salon.

Keep nails short and squared. Avoid acrylic nails, "artwork" decals, and any other artificial add-on that your salon tries to persuade you is the au courant thing. Look au naturel by adding a coat of clear polish. Or faux au naturel with a French pedi. Have your girlfriends over for an in-home spa day and paint each other's nails. This = female bonding plus frugalista savings, and on your own terms.

SAVVY SOURCE FOR FURTHER EXPLORATION
Butterlondon.com

Waxing

Brows and bikinis. A little wax goes a long way. I'm always amazed at how quickly and cheaply a professional can reshape my brows and send me on my merry way. Concerned about the cost? Go quarterly and learn to maintain in-between professional pulls. For your bikini area, how much to remove is a deeply personal decision. The good news is that, with each waxing, the hair seems to grow back a little less intensely. Forgo shaving, as you're sure to get yucky red bumps and need to shave again within a day or so. Nothing is worse than a prickly bikini line. Some health stores have great cold-wax strips for the bikini line that make waxing a breeze. It's not quite the full shebang, but it gets you bikini-ready without an appointment.

85

Skin Care

You can tell much about a person's lifestyle from the texture of her skin. Did she indulge in tanning beds during the nineties? Develop a smoking habit in college? Sip soda rather than water? All of these habits play out on our exterior. As an early adopter of a skin care obsession, I've slathered myself nightly in heavy creams and can't sleep without water by my bed. To keep skin looking fresh, invest in healthy habits. Here are a few suggestions:

- Wash morning and night with a gentle cleanser that has not, of course, been tested on animals.

- Drink oodles of water. Tap water is now superchic, prevents plastic waste, and saves money! Next, drink more water.
- Get plenty of shut-eye.
- Dab on eye cream. Dot under your eyes until fully absorbed.
- Spritz your face with a refreshing rosewater or lavender mist. Pure bliss.
- Invest in a full-service facial four times a year. Yes, extractions and all.
- Shield yourself from the sun. Use a day moisturizer that contains sunscreen. Don your Jackie Os and a big straw hat to boot.
- Eat your fruits and veggies. These little gems will hydrate you from the inside out.
- Bathe in moisturizer nightly. Sure you may feel like a greased monkey, but your skin will sing with glee.
- Douse your body with sesame or coconut oil infused with lavender before your shower each morning to indulge in *abhyanga* — an Ayurvedic oil massage. Dip your fingers into the massage oil and apply all over your body. Wait ten to fifteen minutes to let it absorb, and follow with a relaxing warm bath or shower.

DECLARE BED DAY

A few years ago I started a minirevolution. Every other month or so, I would stay in bed for an entire Sunday and declare it "bed day." Sure, I could bring in my laptop, planner, or any other tool to keep me productive, but the point was to nest and relish having no plans. For a planner like me, this is a huge accomplishment. Recently I declared myself a bed day dropout when I wasn't able to stay in bed later than 2 PM. I grew anxious and felt guilty, so I headed to the theater and bookstore instead. Overall, there are no rules for bed day, only the intention to stay in bed. Here are some tips to ensuring a successful bed day extravaganza:

- Don your comfiest loungewear, whatever won't scream "pajamas," in case you receive an unexpected delivery or houseguest.
- Brew a pot of tea and place it bedside.
- Light a scented soy candle when the day begins. Blow it out when your bed day is over.
- Light your aromatherapy burner, and keep your stash of essential oils nearby for variety and replenishing.
- If you're addicted to being connected, place your cell phone and laptop nearby so you won't be tempted to leave the bed to check them.
- Play inspiring tunes in the background.
- Have a carafe of water infused with mint leaves and strawberries handy.
- Surround yourself with at least five books that you are currently reading.
- Have a bowl of almonds mixed with dried cranberries nearby — vitamin E and vitamin C.
- Keep your journal and/or idea book close at hand to jot down inspirations as they arise.
- Declare the bed a makeup-free zone, but moisturizer, a dab of *huile de parfum* behind the ears, and lip balm are musts.
- Lose track of time. Declare bed day only on days when you have no other obligations. Time is irrelevant.
- Invite your furry companions. Everyday is bed day for them. Follow in their paw prints.

87

SOLITUDE

Considering that I live with a beau, two furry felines, and one beloved pug in six hundred square feet, and spend a lot of time working at my yoga studio, which can have over a hundred yogis buzzing about, I treasure my time alone. With people always around — such as coworkers, spouses, offspring and/or others — it's a wonder most women aren't running for the hills seeking solitude. Anne Morrow Lindbergh wrote an amazing book about the need for solitude called *Gift from the Sea*. Every woman should own it and memorize passages from it.

Notice your reaction to silence and being alone. Do you fill it with TV or music? Do you call long-lost girlfriends or spend a lot of time online? Can you get comfortable being all by yourself? It may take some getting used to, but it allows you to connect to parts of yourself that you may keep hidden — even from yourself. Alone time offers the perfect opportunity to explore your spiritual side. Get to know its nature.

OOH LA LA, ALONE TIME

Still not convinced? Here is an inexhaustive list of what to do with solitude: sleep, knit a beret, sew a skirt, dance to house music, read, start your novel, cook a fancy feast for one, draw your ideal life, write a business plan, meditate, soak in the tub, garden, play with your pet, organize your closets, nap, daydream, doodle, make a collage, reflect, play an instrument, practice yoga, blog, rearrange furniture, be an armchair traveler, listen to Bach, write a letter, bead a necklace, tidy your lingerie drawer, paint your toenails, listen to a classic book on tape, download a financial podcast, mix your own green cleaning products, don a face mask, dabble with charcoal or pastels, plan a party, indulge in an Audrey Hepburn film fest.

JET-SET IN STYLE

Getting from city to city in style is not for the faint of heart. Careful planning, strategic packing, and a flexible attitude are critical for today's traveler. There will be delays, lost luggage, wrong turns, and language barriers. However, indulging the travel bug is sure to launch you into a changed reality. Here's an assortment of travel tips:

SAVOR A STAYCATION. It may seem odd to start a travel section with a focus on staying home, but I find that this concept fits all pocketbooks and lifestyles. Hole up at home reading books you've eyed on your shelves for years. Sleep in without any checkout time or early morning housekeeping service knocks. Be a tourist in your own town — explore the local library, museums, art galleries, and cafés.

GO SOMEWHERE ELSE, BUT PACK LIGHTLY. Considering that we now pay a pretty penny to take luggage on a plane, it makes sense to travel as simply as possible. Pack staples that can easily be mixed and matched to make multiple outfits, accessories that will assist with dressing up or down, a reusable water bottle, cell phone and laptop (don't forget the chargers), lingerie, digital camera, journal with pens, toiletries, two intoxicating books, and a soy travel candle with matches.

CONSIDER YOUR MOTHER. Mother Earth, that is. Remember your commitment to green living while respecting and exploring other cultures. Choose green hotels, when possible — Kimpton Hotels have won my heart because they are swanky and pet-friendly. Forgo having the bed changed and towels washed daily. Tote your reusable water bottle. Leave the environment as you found it — maybe even better by hauling out any pesky litter. Go on a road

SAVVY SOURCE FOR FURTHER EXPLORATION
Treesftf.org

trip in a hybrid car. Take a weeklong bicycle trip through your nearby forest or national park. If you must jaunt far, offset your plane's carbon emissions by planting trees (or an entire forest) through Trees for the Future.

DRESS FOR THE JOURNEY. Comfort is key if you are going to be plane or car bound for hours at a time. I consistently don black palazzos or leggings and slip-ons such as ballet slippers, which allow me to sit cross-legged comfortably, along with fitted top layers to adjust to changing climates, and take a throw to hide my lap-loving pug during long flights. My Klean Kanteen, lip balm, rosewater facial spritzer, and moist towelettes ensure I stay hydrated and refreshed during the voyage. Avoid metal earrings, bangles, or necklaces that will hold you up in security.

DO YOUR RESEARCH. In 1995, when I backpacked through Europe after university, I carried my trusty, five-inch-thick *Let's Go* guide everywhere and was at the mercy of the author's suggestions. Now you can get so much information at your fingertips by exploring everything online. Do your due diligence so that you're sure to find lodging in the area of town where you want to spend the most time (saves on in-city travel fees), determine the sights you want to visit and when (helps prevent the disappointment engendered by CLOSED signs), and learn about the culture before setting foot onto another country's soil. Also be flexible enough to take delight in the unexpected — to walk around without a plan and just take in the scene. And whatever you do, forgo the slouchy jeans, T-shirt, and tennis shoes, no matter how practical and comfortable they may seem.

LA MAISON IN STYLE

Your savvy style goes beyond what you wear and infuses your surroundings. Your home does not need to look like something straight out of the Pottery Barn catalog. It should reflect your personality, your passions, and your concern for the environment.

Forgo Clutter

To showcase your sustainable style at home, start by clearing clutter. Too many baubles detract from the focal point and function of a room. Even if you live in a tiny studio, take the time to put the miscellaneous materials into their proper places. The ancient art of feng shui encourages us to let energy flow freely through our homes, and it is hard for it to do so if there is clutter blocking its movement.

I grew up in a home that contained enough stuff to fill a museum and enough books to start a local library. As I've gotten older, I continually focus on simplifying. Sure, I have a penchant for books, bamboo clothing, and bath products, but keeping these items in their designated spots ensures order in tiny *chez moi*.

SAVVY SOURCE FOR FURTHER EXPLORATION

Gorgeously Green:
8 Simple Steps
to an Earth-Friendly Life,
by Sophie Uliano

Take the time to do seasonal deep cleanings — at least in spring and fall. It's amazing how much you can accumulate, and this offers insight into how little you truly need in order to get through your day-to-day.

Beautify *le Boudoir*

Your bedroom is a sacred space that must be decorated as such. Choose a soothing palette that oozes relaxation. This is your sacred space for reading, sleeping, napping, cuddling, canoodling, and daydreaming in the utmost comfort. Keep any semblance of work at bay. Yes, it's okay to work from bed on occasion, but keep the notion of work out of your boudoir as much as possible. Choose calm lighting — preferably dimmable. A chandelier is always a welcome, girly touch. Have a bedside table with a lamp, stack of books, photo of your beloved (artist, beau, pet), and space for your teacup or flute of bubbly. A fluffy rug and equally fluffy slippers next to the bed are keys to keeping cozy when in need of

WAYS TO KEEP CLUTTER AT BAY, EVEN IN A PETITE SPACE

- If you subscribe to magazines, go through the issues to pull out articles of interest so that you don't accumulate stacks of unread magazines. Drop off read issues at a nursing home or doctor's office.

- Keep your paperwork in pretty, labeled files. Gone are the days of only manila folders. Now you can get aviary-themed, damask, or polka-dot files. Helps make tax documents more fun.

- Avoid overloading flat surfaces such as bookshelves, mantels, bedside tables, kitchen tables, and counters. Revel in empty space.

- Cluster your toiletries together. I have a basket for lip glosses and a basket for all other makeup must-haves, such as eye shadows, powders, sharpeners, mascara, and so on. My loo has five built-in shelves, where I group moisturizers, body lotions, dental care, night creams, leave-in conditioners, and perfumes for easy access.

- As happens in many small spaces, your kitchen table may double as a desk. Try to keep everything on it in one pile (even if that pile is supertall, it will seem more manageable than papers strewn over the entire surface).

- If you aren't blessed with a spacious abode full of nooks and crannies to hide your possessions, consider paring down and investing in an armoire. In the past I have used my armoire as a desk, and now it is storage for stationery; it's also a holding spot for packaged gifts, computer paraphernalia, and boxes of photos; and the top serves as a bed for my beloved feline Bonnard. If guests are coming over, I can quickly transport my kitchen-table "desk" items into the armoire and, voilà, no one knows!

a midnight loo break. Get some greenery — nothing faux, you need living, breathing foliage. The under-the-bed space is best kept free of anything — even a lonely dust bunny. Let any artwork be a reflection of your inner artist, something that beckons you, too, to create. Ensure order within your closets, dressers, and trunks. Line the bottoms of drawers with scented drawer liners. Clutter must be kept to an absolute minimum in this room of restoration.

Sleeping Beauty

Rest is an art, and let's treat it as such. You are a busy lady and replenishing is nonnegotiable. The key is *how* you replenish. To maintain the hustle and bustle during your waking hours, getting adequate sleep is critical — yes, seven to nine hours nightly. Set yourself up for sleeping success by gathering the following accoutrements: eye mask (channel Holly Golightly from *Breakfast at Tiffany's*), earplugs, a source of hydration on the bedside table (water with a mint leaf or lemon slice), pillow spray, lip balm, pen and paper, and a soothing alarm (if you must wake up unnaturally).

Experts encourage keeping the room cool for optimum sleeping conditions. I find that having a pen and paper nearby ensures that I capture the random to-do or idea that comes to me in the middle of the night. That way it isn't lost and doesn't keep me up pondering it. I'm able to write it down and return to dreamland. If you live near a noisy intersection, a white-noise machine or small fan may assist with drowning out the city sounds.

Before crawling into bed, take a moment to do a sun salutation or small ritual to close your day. Write a brief recap of your day. Spill out any lingering thoughts. Try to approach your bed as a sacred space where you leave the past behind and enjoy a fresh slate of sleep.

To that end, ensure that your bedding is ubersoft. Indulge in yummy bamboo or organic cotton sheets. Invest in the highest thread count you can afford. Change your linens weekly. Nothing feels as divine as slipping into fresh bedding for a good night's slumber. Top off the linens with lofty down comforters (I have two, plus a down blanket). For an added dose of luxury, try a down bed (it slides under your fitted sheet) and oodles of pillows for all the staging needed to set up the perfect slumber. I like a pillow under my head, one over my head, another between my knees, and one to cuddle with. Yes, I'm a princess when it comes to my beauty rest.

GET YOUR BEAUTY REST

For those nights when the slumber goddess is not looking kindly upon you, I have a few suggestions to make the most of this unfortunate situation. Have your journal and a pen nearby to help nip any nagging cares or concerns in the bud. If that doesn't work, turn on your bedside lamp, pull out your book-of-the-moment, and begin reading. This will often help you drift into la-la land.

My next ploy is to venture into another room to indulge in a legs-up-the-wall position. This is relaxing and can help rid the mind of whatever is plaguing it at the moment. Another option is to engage in meditation. Set your timer, close your eyes, and focus on your breath. For ladies who struggle to find time to meditate, this found space might be a welcome surprise. Finally, if all else fails, I head to the living room, open my trusty MacBook, and dive into a project. Before too long, my eyes are barely open, and I crawl under the covers for a little more beloved shut-eye.

Keep your boudoir free of TV and work. Making it your personal sanctuary will help your mind settle and begin to relax immediately upon entering. Avoid caffeine (found in tea, coffee, soda, and chocolate) in the later half of your day.

Savor Your *Salle de Bains*

Think of your loo as your personal spa. Keep it clean, welcoming, and beautifully lit. Hang a fluffy robe on your door. Display all your colorful bathing accoutrements — scented soaps, soothing bath salts, moisturizing lotions. Carve out a space for a basket filled with assorted rolled cloths for your guests to dry their hands on. Paper is so passé. Add a soft, absorbent rug for caressing your tootsies pre- and postbath. If space allows, add art to inspire you. I have a beautiful image of a Georgia O'Keeffe orchid in soothing pastels hung across from my mirror.

Bathing Rituals

After the glorious art of sleeping, my favorite pastime is partaking in a long, luxurious soak in the (preferably claw-foot) tub. During the cooler months, you'll find me marinating nightly in some yummy concoction of bath salts, bubble bath, or bath bombs. This is more about indulgence than cleaning *le corps*. You've probably seen the commercial "Calgon, take me away." It may seem silly that the simple act of immersing yourself in water can be touted as producing miraculous results. I'm here to evangelize that water has healing effects; indulging in them is called hydrotherapy. For centuries in European spas, water has been used to release toxins, treat disease, and stimulate blood circulation. Jump right in!

CONSCIOUS COMMUNICATION

Your personal style is evident not only in your clothing and accessories and your personal space but also in the way you connect with others. Let's explore ways to present ourselves in a thoughtful, compassionate, and clear manner.

We communicate constantly through our body language,

BATHTIME BLISS

To turn your bath into a religious experience, gather the following accessories:

- Lavender and eucalyptus Epsom salts
- A bathtub wineglass holder — even your sparkling water will taste better when sipped from a fancy glass
- Inflatable bath pillow
- An assortment of all-natural bath bombs
- White organic cotton plush rug
- Fluffy pink chenille robe for postbath lounging (I've been known to sleep in mine)
- Black chenille ballet flat slippers for postbath lounging
- Soy candles
- Space heater to induce a saunalike vibe
- Washcloth to douse with cool water and keep your brow free from perspiration beads

emails, written memos, and facial expressions, as well as verbally. Ensure that your communications accurately reflect what you want to convey. This simple act can have a profound effect. It will help you avoid misinterpretations or hurt feelings, establish a signature style, and determine how you make others feel when they interact with you. Let's explore my top five communication etiquette tips.

BE CLEAR AND CONCISE. Record yourself speaking. Are *um* and *like* a regular part of your lingo? The way we communicate with others says a lot about who we are. Save your syllables and let go of stammering, which dilutes your point. As a teacher of yoga teachers, I encourage clear and concise cues when instructing a class. The same is necessary in everyday life. Be unmistakable and to the point. Avoid excessive use of *just, sort of, kind of* — remove them from your written communications and notice how much more confident the sentence becomes. Say what you mean, mean what you say. You and those around you will thank you for it. If an email is longer than five or so lines, pick up the phone instead. Use the appropriate means of communication, and know your audience. Your older family members or friends may much prefer a phone call to an email, whereas your teenage niece may prefer that you send a message on Facebook.

ALWAYS SEND THANK-YOUS — preferably via snail mail. Indulge in personalized stationery made of recycled paper, sparkly pens, and a signature closer, such as a wax seal, sticker, or stamp. Taking the time to pen a letter will bring great joy to the recipient whose mail typically consists of bills and unwanted catalogs. A thank-you note should go out within one to two weeks after the receipt of gifts or after events. This tiny courtesy says so much and definitely determines whom I hire, commingle with, and admire.

REMEMBER PEOPLE'S NAMES. We love the sound of our own name. Using it shows that you care enough to remember someone, and can definitely help you stand out in the crowd.

BE BUBBLY. Without throwing in oodles of emoticons, make sure your written communication comes across as loving and as compassionate as possible. Use an exclamation point after "Thanks!" Start your correspondence by thanking the recipient for reaching out. End on a positive note. Answer the phone with a pleasant tone even if you're balancing a child on one hip and a box of legal briefs on the other.

AVOID GOSSIP. This silly banter can produce karmic demerits for those who partake. When I worked at a law firm, I was shocked at how much interest people took in others' misfortunes. Since I know that what goes around, comes around, I did my best to avoid such indulgences and to say something positive about the person in the hot seat. Luckily, as the owner of yoga-related organizations, I don't come across this negativity. But when I hear students or staff complaining about another style or teacher of yoga, I do my best to find something uplifting to say, and then move on. You don't want to be *that* girl: the one you can't trust to honestly express how she feels, but who does so behind your back. There's nothing enlightened about that.

THROW *UNE FÊTE*

The joys of entertaining. Hosting an intimate dinner for two or a cocktail party for fifty can be a beloved pastime for the tranquilista looking to engage in scintillating conversation, work the room, and network. Making the event a stress-free, easy endeavor is all in the initial planning stages. Following is a time-line breakdown for pulling together a seamless event.

98

1. Weeks or months out (depending on soiree size): choose theme, date, and time.

    Send invitations and collect RSVPs.

2. Weeks or days out: begin accumulating dry goods such as candles, candied nuts, cloth napkins, and gifts.

3. Day of: whip up fresh food and purchase flowers (or pick from your garden).

    Clean house, decorate, set a festive table and bar, light candles, pack goody bags, turn on mood music, identify hors d'oeuvres with name cards, and slip into something comfortable.

    Welcome guests, offer beverages, take coats and bags, and let your inner domestic goddess shine.

4. Follow up with a *merci beaucoup* to each guest and photos of the festivities.

NOSH ON NOURISHMENT

Considering I have a penchant for icing-laden cupcakes, it feels insincere to be crafting this section, but a woman cannot live on pastries alone. Believe me, I've tried. The body begs for greens . . . then another cupcake to wash it all down!

Begin by keeping a food diary. Jot down every morsel you take in for an entire week. Yes, even that sliver of dark chocolate your office mate passed along. In addition to what you consumed, note how you felt afterward. Guilty, pure, energized, or drained? This weeklong log will furnish great insights into small changes that you can make to provide your body with its necessary nutrients while still indulging along the way.

I remember a quote from *O* magazine that has stuck with *moi* for almost a decade: "Nothing tastes as good as thin feels." Ah, I'm often guilted into remembering this quote when my simple indulgence quickly turns to gorging on a favorite comfort food. Is the second piece of pie worth an extra hour of sun salutations? It just may be!

99

Sample Menu

BREAKFAST: Steel-cut oats topped with walnuts, bananas, and brown sugar, plus freshly squeezed orange juice.

LUNCH: Veggie wrap stuffed with spinach, tomatoes, dressing, and brown rice or black beans.

MIDDAY SNACK: Clementine, nuts, dried mango, apple, cottage cheese, scoop(s) of peanut or almond butter.

DINNER: Brown rice, yummy steamed greens, side salad, apple crisp.

DAILY ROUTINE

In section 1, we dissected the importance of a morning ritual — starting your day on an intentional note. Now I want to explore ways to carry this intention into your entire day by consciously carving out a routine. Of course, every day is different, and some days may actually feel like they are someone else's life, but it is important to have an inkling of structure to keep you on track.

Humans are creatures of habit, and when you establish a routine you are better able to stay true to your mission. The following is a sample weekly schedule for the well-balanced tranquilista.

Monday through Friday

7–9 AM: Prep: primp, prepare for day, pray.

9 AM–6 PM: Work: deal with emails, work on projects, make calls, connect with team.

6–10 PM: Indulge: eat dinner, do yoga, go to the theater or to an art or language class, answer emails, connect with friends, attend a board meeting.

10–11 PM: Unwind: read a good book, soak in the tub, review tomorrow's to-do list.

11 PM: Turn lights out, don eye pillow.

Saturday and Sunday

9 AM: Rise and shine.

10 AM–6 PM: Do yoga, organize home, grocery shop for the week, work on projects, handle emails and calls, write novel, volunteer, spend time with loved ones.

6 PM: Enjoy social time with family and friends, take in a cultural event, indulge in an indie flick.

GET MOVING

To maintain a svelte figure, supple spine, and sassy attitude, it is critical that you exercise your body every single day. Don't fret,

I'm not declaring a one-hour yoga practice or spinning class, simply some conscious movement to get your heart rate up and stretch your spirit. Following are a few suggestions to explore.

Do Yoga

Of course I had to start here! A sun salutation is a simple, twelve-step process for warming up the body and awakening the mind. *How to sun salute*:

1. Stand at the front edge of your mat and exhale while bringing your hands to prayer position.
2. Inhale and extend your arms over your head.
3. Exhale, swan dive your arms out to the sides, and fold forward.
4. Inhale and step back with your right leg to a lunge position.
5. Exhale and step back with your left leg to the down dog pose.
6. Inhale and float forward to the plank pose.
7. Exhale, drop your knees, bend your arms, hug your elbows in, and keep your shoulders, head, and hips in a straight line as you lower your torso into half-*chaturanga*.
8. Inhale, drop your belly, and slide up to the cobra position.
9. Exhale, curl your toes under, and lift your hips up and back to the down dog position.
10. Inhale and step forward into a lunge with your right foot.
11. Exhale, step your left foot in between both hands, and assume a forward fold.
12. Inhale, swan dive up, and bring the palms of your hands together above your head. Exhale and place your hands in the prayer position.

101

SAVVY SOURCE FOR FURTHER EXPLORATION

Jivamukti Yoga: Practices for Liberating Body and Soul, by Sharon Gannon and David Life

Dance

Turn on your favorite tunes, close the curtains, and let your body go. *How to shimmy*: There are many different types of shimmies. The Egyptian style shimmy is robust, full, and fun. It can be a beautiful and invigorating massage for the belly and whole body. Start with your feet parallel and slightly apart, placed just underneath your hips. Without letting your tailbone tip upward or locking your knees, gently bend first one knee and then the other, as though you're running in place, while keeping the soles of your feet on the ground. Now speed up and alternate as fast as you can. Your hipbones will be still, but the belly and curves of the hips should be soft and jiggling.

Box

When I saw the pink gloves, I knew I had to give this sport a try. I love my weekly sessions, and find boxing to be an amazing cardio workout. The coordination of feet and arms will keep you on your toes. *How to right hook*: From your preferred stance, twist your body sharply to the left at the waist, shifting your weight onto your left foot, and lift your right heel to pivot slightly. Bring your right glove and elbow parallel to the floor as you hit the bag.

Walk

Slip into comfy shoes, skip the bus, and walk your bum to work. *How to walk*: To get your heart rate up, add small hand weights, pump your arms, gradually increase your pace, and head for the hills.

Do Pilates

Connect with your core through a private equipment session or group mat class. *How to do a roll-up*: Rest on your back, and lift and extend your arms in line with your ears, parallel with the floor.

Inhale as you raise your arms and start to roll forward vertebra by vertebra, rounding your back as you go and reaching toward your toes. Inhale again as you begin to uncurl your back, vertebra by vertebra. Tuck your chin, and keep your legs extended. As your arms reach in line with your ears, slowly exhale and roll down to start again. Pause for a moment, and repeat ten times.

Cycle

I tool around town on a white beach cruiser with pink rims and a wicker basket that I bought online. Start with something that fits your lifestyle and feels practical. *How to ride alongside traffic*: Obey traffic laws. Ride with traffic, not against. Stay mindful at all times — avoid talking on your mobile, daydreaming, or checking out people across the street. Make sure you're visible with reflective gear and blinking lights. When possible, take the road less traveled. Ah, and don your helmet. Always.

103

Swim

An amazingly therapeutic workout if you can get past the attire. *How to backstroke*: Float on your back, kick your legs up and down with your toes pointed out. Twist at your waist and windmill your arms pinky-first. As one arm cuts the water, the other arm lifts. Keep your eyes up and your head floating in the water.

STYLISH + SUSTAINABLE

As a girl-on-the-go, you'll find that taking time to nurture your inner and outer selves will have profound effects on how you feel, how you're perceived, and how healthy you stay. Mental and physical health is critical to our ability to create the life we dream about. By putting yourself first, making movement, sleep, and skin care a priority, you are better able to nurture those around you — at work and at home. And, I encourage you to do it all in style — sustainably!

MODEL MUSE

Audrey Hepburn is a fashion icon who exuded grace, elegance, and charisma. Her *Breakfast at Tiffany's* wardrobe turned her into a style sensation: hats, long white gloves, large sunglasses, the little black dress, and pearls continue to be beloved staples among fashionistas everywhere. Audrey was a muse for the designer Givenchy — simple, yet chic. A dancer from an early age, she made ballet flats her signature, along with a crisp white wrap shirt — all very ballet-esque. Her colors were monochromatic — mostly black (*très* chic), beige, or white. Skinny black pants were a must-have. Her legacy continued as she became the face for a 2006 Gap campaign featuring her dancing in the skinny black cigarette pant. Boatnecks, turtlenecks, and shift dresses are also classic Audrey. To top off her incredible style, she had a compassionate heart and spent her later years working for UNICEF as an appointed goodwill ambassador.

SAVVY SOURCE FOR FURTHER EXPLORATION

Audrey Style, by Pamela Clarke Keogh and Hubert de Givenchy

PART 3. DECORATE WITH SPRINKLES

Our Entrepreneurial Topping

6. SAVVY START-UP

If you can create an honorable livelihood, where you take your skills and use them and you earn a living from it, it gives you a sense of freedom and allows you to balance your life the way you want.

— ANITA RODDICK

Ever thought it would be glamorous to be liberated from your corporate cubicle to build your own business, be a sought-after expert, or hone your craft full-time? Ponder these inspiring statistics from the Center for Women's Business Research: One in eleven adult women in America is an entrepreneur; 10.6 million women sell their goods and services while employing 19.1 million people and making $2.5 trillion in sales. It's also true that 1 million people start a business each year, and 40 percent of them will be out of business by the end of the first year; 80 percent will be out of business within five years. Needless to say, launching your own empire is both exciting and risky.

This section of the book is about exploring how to make a living and build a career in an enlightened way. Everything about this concept addresses your situation whether you work for a company, whatever the size, or have a tiny home-based business (or business *dream*) that you're hoping to grow. We'll cover the gamut of details related to professional growth, including time management, logistics, and the fine art of branding. As a serial entrepreneur since 1999, I find this topic to be incredibly energizing. Sit back, kick up your heels, and enjoy this ride!

START SMALL, GROW ORGANICALLY

I'm a staunch supporter of dipping your toes into the water before diving in. For example, my yoga studio, Tranquil Space, launched in my living room, where I had no additional overhead, could test the waters while working my day job, and was able to ensure that Washingtonians were interested in yoga. My clothing company began with a few products before turning into seasonal collections sold in boutiques and spas across the country and in Canada.

Starting a business is taxing enough without also having to worry extensively about certain overhead costs. As I've found myself outgrowing spaces over the years, I've made the necessary changes to take the next step to a larger, more accommodating home. These stepping-stones have helped me avoid additional financial pressures and ensured I didn't have to take out any debilitating business loans ... until my eighth year in business, when I undertook the huge project of renovating an entire three-level building! Gasp.

You may have big dreams for your *bebé* and want to take your business to the next level. I encourage you to fully explore unconventional options. Start a dance studio in a church parlor. Begin to sell your baked goods at an established café, rather than opening your own. Write a few articles for publication before launching into your novel. Sell your handcrafted tees at craft fairs before starting a full-fledged clothing line or boutique. Try your art workshops out at local schools before renting a full-time facility to offer your services.

These simple first steps will allow you to explore your path strategically without getting in over your head. Doing so gives you the opportunity to hone your craft in a smaller capacity and work out the kinks before taking it global.

SAVVY SOURCE FOR FURTHER EXPLORATION

The Girl's Guide to Starting Your Own Business: Candid Advice, Frank Talk, and True Stories for the Successful Entrepreneur, by Caitlin Friedman and Kimberly Yorio

What's Your Vibe?

You have a way about you that is special and different. Honing in on this can do a lot to uncover how you will present yourself to clients, what your work space will look like, what you will offer clients, and the special touches you'll add to your product or service. What makes you unique? Sure, your idea is brilliant, but why is someone going to choose you over a competitor? Pull out your journal and jot down what makes your take on doing business different. Are you good at underpromising and overdelivering? Are you a massage therapist and a psychotherapist able to offer your clients different modalities of treatment? Are

SAVVY SOURCE FOR FURTHER EXPLORATION

Make a Name for Yourself: Eight Steps Every Woman Needs to Create a Personal Brand Strategy for Success, by Robin Fisher Roffer

you a business coach who has run multiple companies over the years? Are you a stay-at-home mom eager to create a community of local moms?

109

My biggest drive when starting Tranquil Space was to create a sense of community — think Norm in the TV show *Cheers* sans drink. I envisioned a place to mingle with like-minded people and feel part of something special. This intention has translated into each of my subsequent businesses. I was heartened to hear during a recent team retreat that the Tranquil Space team noted "community" as their favorite thing about the studio.

Attend to the Legalese and Logistics

Here's some not-so-sexy stuff that is critical to your business setup. When mentoring entrepreneurial wannabes, I always encourage consideration of the following.

REGISTER YOUR TRADEMARK. As a former trademark paralegal, I feel strongly about the importance of securing your brand through this simple (we hope) process. After brainstorming, do a quick search at Uspto.gov to see if your beloved name is available. Once you're set on your brand name, consult an attorney who specializes in intellectual property — ideally trademarks — and get your brand on the books.

GET YOUR EIN. Think Social Security number for your business. An employer identification number is easy to get (and free) through IRS.gov.

DETERMINE YOUR LEGAL STRUCTURE AND GET LEGIT. All my businesses are limited liability companies, except the nonprofit — which is a whole other can of paperwork worms. Your decision here affects your personal liability and the taxes you'll be paying, so do your research and speak with an attorney or accountant who specializes in small businesses. File all local business paperwork to make your organization legit. An attorney can help you maneuver the bureaucratic nightmare, where you may, sadly, spin your wheels if you go about it on your own.

SET UP A BUSINESS BANK ACCOUNT. You usually need your EIN and documentation of your legal structure to set up your account. Do this as quickly as possible, because separating your personal and business income and expenses at tax time is never pretty, and you may have an unhappy accountant on your hands if you arrive with a Manolo box full of receipts!

GET A SEPARATE CREDIT CARD. Yes, I feel silly checking out at a store when I have four separate transactions for three businesses and my personal needs, but it makes the accounting easier down the road. Begin using a separate credit card to track all supply purchases, business lunches, gifts for clients, and business-related needs.

BUY INSURANCE. Get liability, health, worker's comp (if you have a staff), disability (key for sole proprietors), and property insurance. Find a trusted insurance broker, and don't open your doors until you're covered with a good liability policy. Our society is much too litigious to take these risks.

SET UP A GOOD FILING SYSTEM. I prefer colorful files with pretty labels. The key is to have a file for each document category (insurance policies, bank statements, business plan, credit card statements, legal documents) that is easily accessible. Paper clip all credit card receipts to your statements, and your accountant will express glee over your organizational skills.

ACQUIRE A SALES TAX LICENSE. Also called a certificate of resale. If you're selling products, the state government wants its cut, so get the proper paperwork at their office. Your local government may also require a business license, so don't forget that "fun" paperwork while you're down there.

111

MAKE CONTRACTS FOR YOUR AGREEMENTS. When doing business with a new client, vendor, possible partner, contractor, landlord, new hire — anyone — be sure to get your expectations and what you agree to in writing. No exceptions. Yes, even if your mother is making your products. Memory only goes so far, and having clear expectations helps prevent a ton of headaches down the road. Trust *moi*!

GET A SEPARATE PHONE LINE. A business line is usually much more expensive than a standard home line, so many people use their cell phones for business these days. May I suggest, however, that you not answer an unrecognized number during a night out on the town? Unless you're a booking agent for rock stars, it doesn't come across as uberprofessional. Plus, the customer wanting to return an item that doesn't fit may be royally confused, since she was expecting voicemail at that hour.

DECIDE WHETHER TO PARTNER OR NOT TO PARTNER. From the get-go, I was told not to partner because it was like a marriage where visions could easily shift, leaving those involved frustrated. Having a partner is an enticing proposition, especially when you realize all the work that goes into building a business. Why not share the workload? However, sharing the responsibilities is never as fluid as it seems and can involve an amazing amount of emotional energy. If you're tempted to explore this option, be sure to clarify in writing who is responsible for what, what your standards are, and how you will end the partnership should it go awry, *before* moving forward.

112

Set a Budget

You may want a plethora of fancy accoutrements when you launch, but assess what you truly need to make your business happen. When I started Tranquil Space, I made a list of the items I needed in order to hold yoga classes: sign-in sheets, a notebook to track calls and registrations, new student forms, schedules, fliers to post around town, business cards, yoga mats, yoga blankets, teacups, tea serving tray and thermos, cookies, music player, and eye pillows. My overhead expenses were low when I launched, since I started the studio at home — rent and utilities were already paid. I used money from my savings to invest in the necessary yoga props and operated this way for almost a year before taking the leap into renting space in a beautiful church parlor with dark wood and lots of light. My budget for launching was small — around five hundred dollars. These humble beginnings allowed the studio to grow into its latest home (and fourth reincarnation), which represents over six hundred thousand dollars in build-out expenses.

Get clear on what you are willing (and can afford) to invest in your new baby. Outline the must-haves (for example, yoga mats and website) and the would-be-nices (for example, yoga props and silver tea tray) to determine your budget. From there, determine what to purchase first, what to look for at secondhand shops (I've found great items to furnish my businesses at these hidden gems), what to barter (design work in exchange for your product or service), and what to add to a future wish list.

SAVVY SOURCE FOR FURTHER EXPLORATION

U R a Brand: How Smart People Brand Themselves for Business Success, by Catherine Kaputa

BRANDING, BABY

This is the exciting part of building a business, or a practice within an existing business. Finally the good stuff, right? I can't tell you how much I love this part. Keep reading; this is where it gets juicy!

Your brand is everything you do to promote your business. From your logo to your website to the colors and font you choose in your print and online materials. It's the overall feel of your product or service.

A Picture Says a Thousand Words: Logo

Your logo is an important indicator of your brand. Think Starbucks. Nike. Apple. Chanel. Polo. Hip Tranquil Chick (ha!). You know these brands when you see their logos. They've done a brilliant job in establishing their brands within a competitive market. Choosing your business name and logo is like choosing the name of your firstborn or your new puppy. This is a very important decision, and it's critical to think it through thoroughly.

The goddesslike logo for Tranquil Space came after many unapproved logo renditions by a graphic designer/yoga student. After not feeling the lotus, yoga pose, and various other logos she pulled together, I came across my current logo while meditating near candles at an event one autumnal equinox. I asked to borrow the candleholder from the facilitator and brought it back to my designer. We added the heart and star to the image and, voilà, a logo was born! I got stuck on the signature font Spumoni (found primarily at ice cream shops, children's hospitals, and . . . yoga studios) and have been using it in promotional materials ever since.

To determine your logo, reflect on what you want to present to your clients. Write down the following: colors you like, images you like, logos you admire, and the emotion you want to evoke. Work with a trusted graphic designer to help bring it to life. Don't settle on a design until you love it. This is an important part of your brand identity. You'll know it when you see it. Make it classic, able to withstand trends. Ensure that it looks fabulous in black and white for newspaper and basic printing. Once finalized, get it to a trademark attorney to make it your own.

114

Website

This is your business card for the whole world to see. My first website was created in exchange for an eighty-dollar yoga class pass. The designer then trained me on basic HTML coding (yikes!), and I was the webmaster for the next two years. Dig into the archives and you'll see why I no longer pursue that endeavor. Now I have the website redesigned at least every two years. We've kept the same colors, logo, and font, but continually update it to give the brand a fresh look while staying true to our roots. When

SAVVY SOURCE FOR FURTHER EXPLORATION
Hostway.com

sitting down to work with a designer, you may experience sticker shock because websites are not inexpensive, but you should be able to get a beautiful basic one designed for fifteen hundred to three thousand dollars. Make sure the domain is your business name or something similar enough. I've decided against using certain business names simply because I couldn't get the .com addresses to go with them.

To determine your look, review other sites and note the URLs so your designer can get a sense of your style. Be sure to list colors, fonts, images, and overall feel. The main components for a website are the homepage and pages for "About Us," a list of products or services with pricing, testimonials, a blog, a press section, retailers who sell your products (if applicable), a newsletter sign-up, and "Contact Us." Tell a story and invite clients in to play.

Printed Materials

By "materials," I mean your packaging (for products), brochures, business cards, store signage, catalogs, stationery, letterhead, and invoices. Make sure that all of the materials evoke the story you wish to convey. Colors, fonts, look, and overall feel must be consistent and uberprofessional. When printing your materials, be green and go with recycled paper and environmentally friendly inks, when possible. As a yoga studio owner, or when donning any of the other professional hats that I wear, I've never needed letterhead. When typing letters or sending invoices, I simply insert a logo into the document and hit print or send. However, if you're launching a solo law practice, letterhead is *très* important. No need to go overboard on materials; just ensure you have the basics to launch and to support your clients' needs.

115

SAVVY SOURCE FOR FURTHER EXPLORATION
Angelprint.com

Tagline

As if choosing a name and logo isn't taxing enough, it's also helpful to have a catchy tagline that describes your business with one pithy statement. For my studios, it's "Uncover your own tranquil space within." This conveys the essence of what I'm hoping to evoke when you enter the space. You may choose a less descriptive, made-up word such as *Kinko's*, *Tranquilista*, or *Kodak* for your trademark. These words are great from a trademarking perspective because they are original and not descriptive, but to go along with a name like this you need something else that imparts the essence of what you are doing. That is where a tagline can come in handy. What pithy phrase encompasses your offering?

Experience

When defining your brand, crystallize the experience you want to create. What emotion do you want stirred up when people come into your space, buy your product, consult with you on the phone, or interact with you or your business in any way? This is essential. For example, I've chosen light colors to brand Tranquil Space in the hope of evoking a state of tranquility. For my logo, I chose a goddess reaching for a star, with a clearly defined heart, to suggest empowerment and reaching for dreams with an open heart. The words *tranquil space* connote a feeling of being nurtured, coddled, and brought to a state of peace. Take a moment to write out what it is you want your business to convey. Values, adjectives, emotions, colors — all these make up the experience.

One last soapbox musing: you must make the experience consistent... always, no exceptions. The key is to write out procedures and processes once you have them down and they feel authentic. This ensures that every time clients call, come to your store, or interact with your company in any way, they know what to expect and they get what they expect. This one nugget is the most important piece of designing and sustaining a business. Commit it to memory: create a consistent, full sensory experience.

Systems

Taking the time to set up standard operating procedures is critical to the success and longevity of your business. Outline such things as how to answer the phone, how to greet clients, what to include when shipping products, how to teach a class, how to hire a new intern, and what information you need from clients to ensure that standards are met, procedures are followed, and consistency is conveyed.

Sit down with pen and paper or your laptop and brainstorm the various processes you have in your business. Then outline in clear and concise instructions how you want each process handled. Begin by writing what you do every day — make a list of everything required to run your business. Then break the list into steps. For example, if one of your activities is to write a blog, outline how you write and post a blog entry. Record a video or take photos of the steps involved. Build your procedures.

Checklists can be extremely helpful tools, too. For example, if you have an upcoming event, you may want to have a time-line breakdown for the event, such as what you do one month before, one week before, day before, and day of, and what you do to follow up. Under each time-line heading, list the various duties, with an associated checkbox for each, to ensure a smooth event. After an event, it's great to sit down with all involved to find out what worked and what didn't work, and to adjust the checklist accordingly so that you can improve your next event. Always debrief.

Checklists ensure consistency so that each time the standard operating procedures are performed, the person doing the work does so in a manner that you want used when dealing with your clients. As you grow, you won't be able to set up for business every day alone, answering the phones, cleaning the floors, stocking the shelves, meeting with clients, maintaining inventory, and shipping products. By setting up these standard operating procedures (and reevaluating them regularly), you are better able to oversee your brand and keep it consistent with your values. This allows you to set up additional locations, go on vacation, or hire new staff who

SAVVY SOURCE FOR FURTHER EXPLORATION

The E-Myth Revisited: Why Most Small Businesses Don't Work and What to Do About It, by Michael E. Gerber

117

can carry out your business in the same way your clients have come to expect.

SELF-MANAGEMENT

Ah, an incredibly important topic that I continue to struggle with despite being in business for a decade now. Managing myself! Ever have moments of reading an entire book, finishing it, and having no idea what you just read? Well, try that with days. You've worked from sunup to sundown, yet you are not sure what you actually accomplished or where your time went. That has been an ongoing saga of mine and tends to be common among entrepreneurs. As a paralegal, I used to track my time in ten-minute increments. Now I can go ten hours and wonder where the day went. Despite my continual struggle, I have found some ways to help rein in the desire to do "just one more thing" before signing off for the day way past my bedtime.

TIME & TO-DO MANAGEMENT

I was introduced to the Planner Pad by a friend a few years ago who saw me struggling with a small planner stuffed with Post-its.

SAVVY SOURCE FOR FURTHER EXPLORATION
Plannerpads.com

This system has literally changed my organizational life. I've always been an organizer (I used to glean great pleasure in organizing the local department store's toy aisle when I was growing up), but this organizational tool took it to a whole new level. As you may know from David Allen's bestseller *Getting Things Done*, it is crucial to get what is in your head down on paper. You must capture ideas and to-dos. They are fleeting and will come back to haunt you after your deadline if you don't write them down.

If you don't have the Planner Pad itself, here's the skinny on why it works so well and how you can set up your own version of it with a basic spiral-bound notebook. In this planner, the two-page spread for each week is divided into three large rows. The top row is for keeping various lists, and the bottom two are specific for noting to-dos and appointments for each day of the week. In my Planner Pad, I use the top row for the to-do lists for my four organizations: Tranquil Space, Hip Tranquil Ventures, TranquiliT, and Tranquil Space Foundation. (Your lists might have headings like Projects, Follow-Up, Family, Clients, Volunteer, Blog, To Order, To Contact, and so on.) Next to those four lists, I have a personal list for things like "make hair appointment," "take puppy to the vet," "create birthday gift for BFF," and so on, and lists for meetings that week, in which I outline the various items to address in those meetings. The idea with this system is that the lists funnel down into the big middle row of the two-page spread, where you note the day's to-dos, and then to the big final row at the bottom, where you note your day's appointments. Genius!

119

I carry my planner everywhere I go. I'm addicted. This system allows me to capture ideas, schedule appointments, and track to-dos. Religiously on Sunday night, I light a candle, nestle into my chaise, and set up the week ahead by reviewing the previous week's ideas and to-dos. I transfer over what I didn't yet get to, and I suss out the week ahead. An item carried over week after week is clearly not making it as a priority, so I evaluate whether it is worth keeping, or whether I can delegate the task. I also set three to five key results that I must accomplish that week. These usually entail events or large projects that I want to ensure are completed by the week's end. Once I've determined these key results, the plethora of mini to-dos that always come up, as well as the random fires that must be put out, can be worked around these larger must-dos. The planner is a tool that helps me focus when I'm bombarded with urgent tasks, calls, and meetings.

To-dos can be overwhelming and unending and may feel like a continual thorn in your side. A few years ago, during a late-night meeting, I was complaining about all I had to do, and the fact that

I was heading back to the office to finish up, when a friend informed me that I would never be done with to-dos. Really? For some reason that was an eye-opening statement. I'd been struggling for years to accomplish all the to-dos that I could. Why bother? There will be more tomorrow, so do your best and call it a day.

I feel the same way with email. Some people thrive on having an empty in-box, but I'm happy when mine has around 70 unanswered messages, and get uncomfortable when it goes over 120. As with to-dos, emails will continue to come even while you sleep, so just do what you can to file the ones you need to reference, handle the ones that take less than two minutes, set aside time to answer ones that take more than two minutes, and delete (and unsubscribe) from those that are not relevant. If you feel like you belong in Email Anonymous, try to wean yourself off the crackberry checking, and limit it to a few select times each day. This will allow you to focus without interruption on getting your key results.

SAVVY SOURCE FOR FURTHER EXPLORATION

Never Check E-mail in the Morning: And Other Unexpected Strategies for Making Your Work Life Work, by Julie Morgenstern

120

IDEA BOOK

To capture ideas while on the go — at lunches, intimate gatherings, or conferences, or while browsing at a bookstore — I always carry a small notebook. Currently it is a small damask notebook stuffed full of ideas that have come to me during various moments over the past months. These small idea books contain a year's worth of musings and are stored in a safe place when finished. I transfer ideas-turned-into-to-dos to my Planner Pad on a regular basis.

Energizer Bunny

Knowing when to stop has never been one of my strong suits. An ongoing goal of mine has been to have a day off and to keep my "Creative Fridays" sacred. I stress my use of the word *ongoing*. After a decade of running at this pace, I have come up with a few parameters to help keep me, and my energy, in check. Facing burnout or exhaustion is not pretty — for you, your clients, your team, or those poor souls who are inhabiting your space. Treat yourself as you would a beloved member of your team — give yourself rewards, time off, and kudos.

Just as you must replenish yourself so that your creativity will flow, you must also fill your entrepreneurial well. Here are my favorite ways to bask in being my own boss while rejuvenating and staying inspired:

- Get a massage, wax, mani, pedi, or hair coloring.
- Shop.
- Go to a matinee.
- Attend industry-related conferences.
- Take a trip to NYC for some top-notch yoga or market research.
- Head to a café to write.
- Take personal development workshops.
- Read, read, and read some more.
- Set boundaries on your accessibility.
- Browse a bookstore while the rest of the city is at work.
- Meet up with a friend for an art exhibit.
- Take yoga, dance, French, or writing classes during the weekday.
- Set a bed day.
- Go on a retreat.
- Take a midday run or walk to clear your head.

The great thing about doing all this on a weekday is that most of the population is at work, so you have appointments, grocery stores, art galleries, and dance classes to yourself. Honestly, this may be reason enough to become your own boss! But one challenge in working for yourself is that work stays on your mind 24/7. You can't gleefully leave a desk of pending projects each night like you did when you were working for someone else. As an entrepreneur you take on a whole different (and heavy) burden.

A few other ideas to keep your energy flowing:

- Sustain yourself. Ensure that your fridge is stocked with heaps of quick and easy, but healthy, food. I'm a fan of organic frozen foods, as I like instant gratification and have little patience.
- Stretch yourself. Get up regularly from your computer for a stretch break.
- Schedule dates. This may seem obvious, but when your next free date is in three months (and it's not because you're rolling in social invites), it is time to reevaluate your usage of time.
- Take play dates. Head to the hills to see fall foliage. Take a class on a topic you've always found fascinating. Go for an afternoon bike ride to clear your head.
- Stay connected. Remember birthdays, send thank-yous, and give kudos.

When you "birth" a business, you may lose sight of the periphery around you. It's normal. But I encourage you to be *abnormal* and go the extra mile to take care of yourself, your relationships, and your mind, which longs for stretches of play coupled with downtime.

BE THE BRAND

This heading sounds so corporate, but I mean this in a very all-encompassing lifestyle way. Ideally, whatever you do for a living

OFFICE YOGA

Taking a moment to open up your body after continuous work at your desk is critical self-care. Here are a few of my favorite stretches to keep my mind and body supple:

- Take ten deep, slow breaths.
- Lower your neck to the right, drop your chin to your chest, and your left ear to your left shoulder. Repeat this U-shaped movement with your head at least five times.
- Interlace your hands behind your back, lift your arms up, and sway from side to side.
- Bring your left hand to your right knee and your right hand to the chair back for a seated twist. Gaze over your right shoulder, take five breaths here, return to center, and repeat on the other side.

123

is an integral part of your life and who you are. That means that you incorporate it into your thoughts, words, and actions. For example, if you run a consignment boutique, it would behoove you to wear clothing from the boutique and always look your best. If you are on the board of a green nonprofit, it is important that you incorporate greening practices into your everyday actions. If you own a stationery store, it would benefit you to send the most luxe invites to your soirees on custom, recycled paper note cards printed with soy ink.

Let your lifestyle and business revolve around your values. Try not to separate them. Separating work and life is a foreign concept for entrepreneurs. If you make a living doing what you love, you will not have the separation that a typical nine-to-fiver may feel. Make choices that align with the values you project in your business and vice versa. This will allow you to be the same person at home, at work, and on the go. We are not such compartmentalized beings that what is important to us in one area of our lives should be ignored in another area. Bring your passions to the forefront and let them infuse all your decisions and the way you present yourself to the world.

START-UP SANITY

As you bring your baby into the world, don't forget to take care of you. Starting a business is incredibly exciting, and the journey will fuel you in a way you may never have experienced before. You will literally eat, sleep, and breathe your enterprise, especially during start-up. Be sure to indulge in a sampling of the self-care suggestions outlined in this section to keep yourself in top-notch form. This will allow you to operate your business with oodles of energy, enthusiasm, and innovation — all critical for your on-going success with enlightened work.

124

MODEL MUSE

Girl Scouts founder Juliette Gordon Low inspires me to dream and think big. Upon meeting the founder of the Boy Scouts, Juliette recognized her calling, and in 1912 she gathered eighteen girls and launched the Girl Scouts. She focused her mission on helping girls get outside, explore roles beyond traditional homemaking, and engage in community service. Juliette was deaf and welcomed girls with disabilities into the organization — which was somewhat avant-garde for her time. Her soul-searching paid off in huge dividends — the organization she started now boasts a membership of 3.4 million! This visionary's start-up effort is still inspiring girls everywhere to make the world a better place. Learn more at Girlscouts.org.

7. BLISSFUL BUILDING

We must have a theme, a goal, a purpose in our lives. If you don't know where you're aiming, you don't have a goal. My goal is to live my life in such a way that when I die, someone can say, she cared.

— MARY KAY ASH

Moving beyond start-up can be scary and exhilarating at the same time. Bookshelves overflow with ideas on starting a business, but information on the actual running and expanding of a business is less readily available. Blissful building is about watching the seeds you've planted grow, cultivating the soil, and making things happen. Throughout this section we'll address ways to grow in a mindful, sustainable way that makes a difference to your community.

SPREAD THE WORD

Getting your name out can be a joyful journey toward establishing yourself as the go-to person for whatever you offer. There are multiple avenues for making this happen, and I'll outline a few that have proven beneficial to me over the past decade.

Network Even If You'd Rather Nest

If you're an introvert, the term *networking* may make you want to curl up at home with a good book. There are a few ways to put yourself out there that feel natural and authentic. Check out a few professional or field-related groups. Drop in on some meetings and see how the vibe feels. Take your business cards. Introduce yourself confidently. Reach out to people you admire and invite them to lunch or tea. Comment on the blogs of like-minded individuals. Follow them on Twitter (more on this later). Join organizations that you've tested and that feel right. Consistently showing up will allow you to build relationships.

Connect with rainmakers who have a knack for networking. That way you can meet people through them without having to do all the work — especially if networking wears you out. Learn to engage in small talk. This is one of the most challenging aspects of networking, but it will propel you to new heights. Ask people about themselves, discuss ideas, and avoid excessive talk about yourself. Be complimentary, smile, listen well, remember names, and follow up.

When you receive a business card, jot a note on the back about something that came out of your conversation with the person, such as "likes to travel," "knits," "has three children." That way when you follow up with a "Nice to meet you" email, you can acknowledge something from your conversation. Note birthdays and send nice notes. Stay in touch with occasional emails, and keep your acquaintances aware of your journey. Avoid spamming your contacts, but touch them electronically a few times a year so you, and your work, stay on their radar.

Speak Your Mind

Over the years I've been asked to speak at universities, women's groups, and business conferences and have accepted every opportunity. These have not typically been paid presentations, and I have yet to get training as a speaker, but I love the chance to share my story with hopes of inspiring others. I usually bring studio schedules, my book, or even my clothing line to help spread the message of tranquility, so this platform gives me a chance to share my work with others.

When you are given that first opportunity to speak to a group of people, I encourage you to jump on it. Sure, you'll be nervous and may wonder what you have to say, but I promise that, with a few tips and some preparation, you'll be in awe of the words of wisdom that come out of your mouth. Seek out opportunities to share your message. Come up with your top five tips, and look into local organizations that may be interested in having a guest speaker at their next meeting — for example, similarly aligned business associations, women's groups, church groups, sororities, garden clubs, and alumnae associations. Remember, giving a presentation at your book club counts as public speaking and is a chance to share your expertise with others. Here are a few tips to make your presentation shine:

PRESENT WELL. Dress according to the audience and appear confident. Avoid swaying from side to side or repeatedly using *um*. Project your voice to the person farthest away from you. Speak slowly and enunciate clearly. Join a local Toastmasters group.

CONNECT. Smile, make eye contact, and be enthusiastic. Try not to read from a prepared speech — instead, have bullet points and glance at them occasionally. Use appropriate humor.

BE PREPARED. Know your subject and your audience. Start with an introduction, move into the body of your talk, and summarize at the end. Rehearse before presenting. Then rehearse again.

BE GRACIOUS. Thank the audience and your host. Offer time for Q & A if that is appropriate, and end with a wrap-up. Share additional resources on the topic. Have handouts that summarize your message, and share takeaway tips.

Speaking is a skill, and every time you accept an opportunity to share, you are able to hone the craft.

HOW TO MAKE A MEMORABLE APPEARANCE

So this may not be in the cards just yet, but as you put yourself out there more, you will be invited to various events and, hopefully, will be the feature of some. Here are a few tricks to make sure your appearance is a showstopper even if you aren't feeling like a star: Remember the adage "act as if" and present yourself as a famous rock star (even if only two people show up). Prepare fully and have automatic, authentic responses to the typical questions, such as "Why did you write this book?" Dress the part — look fabulous and be the persona.

Dish up inspiration through your presentation, interactions with others, and body language. Give the audience more than they expect: a small trinket, takeaway tips, and photo ops — more than just your signature in their book. These additional touches can go a long way. It's critical for you to be "on" at these events. Even if you had a horrible day, are jet-lagged, and feel a cold coming on, put your best face forward. People have taken time out of their busy schedules to see and support you. One final tip if you're on the shy side — break into making appearances by taking part in a panel, so the spotlight isn't only on you. This is a great way to get your feet wet without all the pressure.

Write Your Story

Putting your words into print is a promising way to shape your message and share your work. When I first launched Tranquil Space, I looked for every opening to publish my top five tips for tranquility — from my sorority alumnae publication to small local newsletters and newspapers. This allowed me to dip my toes into the publishing world, see my name in print (always exciting), and share my ideas with people I wasn't yet connected to. If you dream of writing a book or screenplay, now is the time to start sharing your voice with the world. This will help establish you as an expert and increase your knowledge on the topic.

Start with a blog, your top five tips for a community publication, an op-ed piece for the paper, a "lessons learned" blurb for a trade publication or newsletter, or a review of a retreat, product, or restaurant for a magazine or online community. It doesn't matter *what* you start with; the key is to begin getting your voice out there.

START A BLOG

You can send your opinions, tips, photos, art, and ideas around the globe in a matter of minutes. Here are a few simple steps:

1. Determine your message. Do you want this to be professional (industry updates), personal (family photos), informational (recipes, a how-to), or all the above? Is this going to be a pictorial journal of your baby's early years, a daily journal of your life, a blog chock-full of images you find inspirational, a blog about your hobby, or a product review blog? What do you have a lot of knowledge and passion about? Choose one main theme.

2. Set up your blog. Choose a name. Mine has evolved from "TranquiliT Thoughts" to "Hip Tranquil Chick" to "Tranquility du Jour." Make sure the theme resonates with the message you hope to share. Check out Blogger.com, LiveJournal.com, and WordPress.com, where you'll find a free platform and many free templates to choose from. Sign up and begin inputting data. Remember, this is public, so be mindful of what you share with the world.

3. Start writing. Address your audience at least weekly, ideally daily, to keep readers interested in coming back for your fresh ideas and fodder.

4. Connect. Reach out to other like-minded bloggers and comment on their blogs; include a link to your blog. Set up an RSS feed so that your readers know when you've published a new post.

Go Glossy

Getting into a glossy is an exciting proposition. List the publications you'd like to write for. It's key to be a reader of the publication so you understand its message and can tweak yours appropriately. Know your audience and write specifically for them. For example, you wouldn't propose a meat-based recipe for *Vegetarian Times* or a Pilates equipment review for *Yoga Journal*. Take a peek at the publication's media kit given to advertisers — you can gain great insights into the demographics of its readers. Next list the ideas you have for an article and clarify which sections of the magazine your ideas would fit best. Look for ideas that are a fresh take on everyday topics. Check out the magazine masthead to get names of department editors, call the magazine to confirm its address, and send your pitch to the appropriate person.

Collect writing clips (copies of other published work with your byline) from your published writing — yes, even your tips on planting bulbs featured in Gramma's garden club newsletter. As you get into larger publications, you can set aside the less prominent clips, but it's best to have something to show. Avoid sending attachments unless they are PDFs — best to direct the editor to a link on your website if you want to share writing clips. Outline your pitch with a pithy phrase in the subject line and propose a unique story or spin. Note that you'll follow up in a couple of weeks, and do so.

I've had pieces published in *Fit Yoga*, *Yoga + Joyful Living*, and *Healing Lifestyles & Spas*, I've taken a magazine writing class through Mediabistro.com, and I continue to explore the exciting world of getting into glossies. My dream is to have a lifestyle column in a fabulous, eco-chic magazine in the future. What are your writing dreams? How can you get started today penning your prose? Proofread, be a stickler when editing, ensure proper spacing between words, and know the difference between *to*, *two*, and *too*. Now get your thoughts onto paper and enlist the support and careful editing skills of a literary friend.

Teach Your Truth

If you want to get better at what you do, start teaching it. I began teaching yoga in 1999 after my first training, and have been training teachers since 2002. I've been through hours of training over the past decade, and I'm constantly reminded of how much more there is to learn. When I teach yoga aficionados, I am challenged to exude the qualities that I preach when training others. I also have to break down what has become second nature to me into understandable pieces. This process helps me return to the basics and cultivate a beginner's mind. Explore teaching opportunities in your field. Lead workshops, hold a retreat, host a teleclass, or launch a series at a community center, university, art or fitness facility, or online.

131

The process is similar to writing. Determine what you're knowledgeable about and what you're passionate about. How can you break this knowledgeable passion down into small steps? When guest teaching at yoga studios, I choose a topic such as "hips" or "spiritual activism" — something very specific —begin with an introduction (this is what we'll be doing and why), proceed to the body of the lesson (the practice or discussion), and finish with a conclusion (a final relaxation and meditation, followed by a themed reading that brings it all together). The process is similar to that of writing a paper or a speech — find your special spin on a standard topic.

It's helpful to collect teaching "clips" as you do with writing. Being able to list the various locations that you've taught at can help support your cred as a teacher. Sure, it may be "Taught art class at an assisted living center," but at least it shows you have some experience.

Host a Retreat

Setting up a retreat is a lot of work, plus lots of reward. It's like having your own party in a new setting, and it's important to treat it as such. Whether you're a painter, Pilates instructor, writer, activist, or scrapbooker, taking a group of people to a different environment can help each of you hone your skills and give you the space needed to focus. Choosing the location is a big decision. It's important to find a place with flexible booking policies such as a transferable deposit (in case you choose a not-so-enticing time of the year — such as August in steamy Mexico when your clients would prefer to escape the heat), and that is easy to get to (so you can avoid the saga of overly complicated, trains-planes-and-automobiles travel — that way, your retreaters won't be exhausted when they arrive). Make sure the resort is responsive (you don't want to be chasing the proprietors down for answers the day before), offers a special deal to the facilitator (free room and board with ten guests, or some small benefit for bringing a group to the place), doesn't require the full amount up front (a 30 to 50 percent deposit is standard, with the final payment due as the retreat gets closer and you have registrants), and handles the food and special needs (having to cook, handle fragile retreaters, and lead the retreat is too much for someone who has any hope of tranquility).

Once you have the location set, it's time to start promoting via your blog, website, classes, and various communities. Design a postcard with tempting photos that you can leave at local establishments. Create an enticing description (who doesn't crave beach time during the chilly months?). Be sure to mention what the retreaters will get out of the experience. Clearly note the pricing, dates, times, and how to register. Accept payment through your website via PayPal or an online shopping cart. Send a welcome letter outlining all the FAQs

SAVVY SOURCE FOR FURTHER EXPLORATION
Paypal.com

as soon as you receive registrations. Retreaters will be eager to make plans, so give them all the information you can on what to bring, how to travel (nearest airport, how to get to the retreat center), and what schedule, meals, and accommodations will be offered. These are the main types of questions that people will have. Prevent an influx of email questions by putting together an informative welcome packet for your retreat.

Leading a retreat is both exhausting and exhilarating. You're basically the go-to person who is "on" the entire time — during meals and classes, in between classes, during travel — and it can take its toll. Schedule downtime for yourself to "refuel" by getting a massage, taking other classes, going for walks alone, or meditating, so that you're able to give the retreaters your very best. Check in with people and make sure they have what they need, are comfortable, and are enjoying themselves. If you hear any grumbling, do what you can to remedy the situation as soon as possible. Infuse lots of small touches into their experience — goody bags, daily gifts, special surprises, handwritten thank-yous, fresh flowers, music, candles.

Getting feedback after a retreat is helpful in gauging how well it went and what changes to make next time. I like to create an online survey through Surveymonkey.com in order to gather and analyze feedback. To top off the experience, reach out to the retreaters, and welcome them back to reality, I send out a thank-you email with photos and a link to the survey as soon as I'm home.

Rock a Workshop

Leading a workshop is a similarly involved endeavor. My first big workshop was an all-day Wild Woman Workshop. You'd think I was planning a wedding with all the effort I put into it. I rented a beautiful space (often used for weddings), brought in heaps of snack food, had music, readings, and multicolored handouts, and offered a full-on experience with yoga, Pilates, dance, and creativity. I had two rates — an all-day rate and a half-day rate for those who couldn't join us for the full day. The event was a huge success and launched me into doing many more workshops with the confidence that I could pull it off. Treat workshops and retreats as your own private party. Yes, it's scary to facilitate and to put yourself out there in this way, but the more you do it, the better you get at it. Promise!

Find a great venue, bring snacks and beverages, give participants more than they expect, be sure to teach what you promised in the promo materials, have a mailing list so you can stay in touch with them and they can stay in touch with each other (if applicable), and bring related products or information about services they may be interested in. Arrive early to set the stage, welcome everyone (or have an assistant on hand who can do so), do groundwork (inform everyone about group rules, where to find bathrooms), provide an agenda, follow the agenda, and provide a follow-up thank-you note and photos, along with a mechanism for giving feedback.

Share Your Expertise

There are various words used to describe the person who works as an advisor to a company or individual, such as *consultant*, *coach*, and *mentor*. Sharing your experience is an empowering opportunity. Again, knowledge and passion are critical here. I feel like a broken record, but I'm sure you've experienced people knowledgeable about a topic who have lost their spark. No need to rain on other people's parades when sharing your wisdom. As you become more prominent in the public eye due to your speaking, writing, and teaching, you may be asked to serve as an advisor. This can be extremely flattering, and your expert advice should not be given away except as part of your karma work on a non-profit board or similar situation. This is an amazing way to help others realize their potential.

In 2009, I was featured in a *U.S. News* online article as a celebrity-style coach, and the article mentioned that the median charge for one hour of life coaching is $200 to $3,500! The expertise you share is valuable, and it is important that you treat it like a business. I have my clients fill out three preconsultation forms, including a credit card authorization form, a client guide (expectations, phone number to call, confirmed time of appointment), and a questionnaire (what is going on, top three things they hope to take away from the session) — this is "omwork" for them to do in advance of our session. Pulling together these documents and sending them to clients in advance of our appointment sets expectations, lays out my fee, allows them the chance to fill me in on their state before our session, and formalizes the process in a playful way.

If you want to begin consulting, it is important to outline what you offer, at what price, and why you should be hired; this should be backed up with your bio and testimonials from other clients. Present this information in a way that projects your personality. If you're appealing to attorneys, the vibe needs to feel more corporate. If you're marketing to creative folks, it's important that your promotional materials (website, business cards, postcards) convey an innovative edge. It helps clients to know that you speak their language. Birds of a feather flock together and understand each other.

MARKETING MAVEN

Once you've created your brand identity through your logo, website, tagline, and trademark, it's time to take your marketing to the next level via online mediums and getting yourself out into the community. I've always found this aspect of running the business to be creative and rewarding. Honoring your clients, donating to local charities, setting up online groups, writing press releases, sending newsletters, and attending industry events are all ways to spread your message and market your organization. Let the festivities begin!

Craft a Newsletter

Send a regular newsletter (daily, weekly, monthly, seasonally) to keep your clients in the know, remind them of your product or service, and inspire them. I've been sending monthly newsletters about my yoga studio for years and find them to be a great way to stay connected. In each issue I include a musing that relates to the time of year, feature a student and team player, outline the yoga pose of the month, provide updates on studio happenings, feature students in their Tranquil Space T-shirts, highlight the spa and boutique, include a coupon that will let clients save on a particular boutique product or service, and note our karma yoga efforts. It's a fairly long document designed in HTML to match our website and is chock-full of information.

136

Give Back

Get out into the community and show them what you've got. We host adoption days for the Humane Society and have their adoption van park in front of the studio on a heavily trafficked weekend with the idea that they will find pets new homes. We also enjoy donating yoga classes to various local organizations' fund-raisers. We help green our world by planting a tree for every yoga class pass and massage purchased, by using bamboo sheets for our massages, and by forgoing plastic water-bottle sales. We've had toiletry and canned food drives. We offer pay-what-you-can yoga classes. We put together teams for various walks, such as Race for the Cure and the AIDS walk. We created our own nonprofit to focus some of our charity efforts, and we have T-shirts that we sell to promote and raise money for the cause. Each month a Tranquil Space teacher offers a charity class to raise money for her chosen cause.

Organize a team to serve food, or share a service you offer, to

CREATE A NOTEWORTHY NEWSLETTER

Create content that entices, informs, and inspires your readers. Choose a template or have your webmaster design one to match your branding materials. Name it something clever that aligns with your brand. Think "museletter," and update it regularly. Have an easily accessible sign-up page on your website or blog. Link to your past editions. Highlight clients in your newsletter. Include images — this helps to break up text and make it more visually appealing. Interviews that include Q & As are fun to read. Request contributions from your team. Inform, don't advertise. Avoid technical jargon. Spell-check and then spell-check again. Assemble an eagle-eye team to assist with editing and proofreading.

SAVVY SOURCE FOR FURTHER EXPLORATION

Find a template at Constantcontact.com

Yes, you want to let your clients know everything you have going on, but be sure to give them some content, too — for example, recipes, how-tos, a yoga sequence, and product reviews. Give public kudos to your team or graduates of a training you've offered. Include names and photos. Have clients send in photos with your product (wearing your clothing, drinking your beverage, writing on your stationery, showing what they made with your supplies) to highlight in the newsletter or company blog. They'll proudly pass the newsletter along to family and friends — ultimately increasing exposure. Feature additional media sources you offer, such as links to videos, podcasts, blogs, and other locations. Have a promotion that you unveil in your newsletter — a challenge, appreciation week, or special savings.

137

those in need. These do-gooding gestures help identify your organization's values and show you care about the community. In enlightened work, I can say that giving back to others is a must-do. And, it does the soul good!

SOCIAL NETWORKING

Building an online community has become a haute topic these days and is a great way to spread your message virally. It started with services such as Friendster, Classmates, and MySpace, which are now passé. Facebook (social network), Idealist (network for a cause), and LinkedIn (business network) seem to be here to stay (at least until the next thing comes along).

To Tweet or Not to Tweet

Where else can you follow Martha Stewart, Thich Nhat Hanh, Barack Obama, and the Beastie Boys all at once? Twitter.com, baby. This allows you to send and read updates ("tweets") of up to 140 characters. To get started, set up an account at Twitter.com. Use your business name if you want to share updates on what is happening within your business — as Whole Foods and Zappos have done. Use your personal name or a clever persona if you'd like this to be about you as a representation of your company. (Follow *moi* at twitter.com/tranquilista.)

138

Post what you're doing, an inspiring quote, or a link to an informative read, and you can have this directly update your Facebook status at the same time! Be witty and appeal to your audience. Some tweets that have gotten great responses for me have been those that announce the receipt of next season's fabric colors, pose a question, or share an inspirational quote. Avoid using Twitter as a platform for constant promotion of sales, blog posts, or links to your offerings. This feels very salesy and will lose followers. Review who your followers are following, and you'll find a group of like-minded people. Update regularly, but not every few minutes or even every hour, as it will feel like spam to your

SAVVY SOURCE FOR FURTHER EXPLORATION

Twitter Power: How to Dominate Your Market One Tweet at a Time, by Joel Comm followers. Encourage people to follow you by noting your Twitter information on your website, in your email signature, and on your blog.

Set up a Facebook Account

Unless you've been in a long meditation the past few years, you've probably heard of Facebook. Facebook is another way to connect online with friends, colleagues, and everyone in between. Many businesses have a Facebook group or fan page, and it's a great idea to set up one for yours. To get started, visit Facebook.com and set up an account. Through Facebook and other such groups you can create events to let your friends and fans know about your goings-on, such as workshops and retreats; invite them to join; and help spread the word virally. Facebook has some unproductive applications, such as "poking" people and random quizzes (for example, "Which rock star are you?"), and I encourage you to limit these. Be strategic in your use of Facebook.

139

Choose your profile photo carefully. Avoid adding photos of you doing anything that would reflect poorly on your business or brand. Use your Wall (a space to write notes that are public) only for items that you want the world to see. For other types of items, send a private message or email instead. Connect with causes close to your heart. This is a great platform for raising money and awareness for causes and sharing this awareness with friends. You can also import notes into Facebook, which is a great feature that, when set up, allows you to coordinate your Facebook page with your blog. When you post on your blog, Facebook gets updated, too!

Get LinkedIn

This social networking group is used for professional connections, rather than personal. Go to Linkedin.com and fill out a profile.

List your credentials, such as affiliations, past employment, and education. Many people add their LinkedIn page link to their email signatures; you give recipients great insights into who you are without having to include your whole bio in the email. Being part of LinkedIn also increases your presence on the Internet, since your profile is public. One interesting feature is the testimonials page, where clients can leave notes on the quality of your work. As Facebook does, LinkedIn will list people you are peripherally connected with that you may want to add to your network.

Create a YouTube Channel

YouTube is a video-sharing community, and setting up your user profile creates a channel where you're the programming director. People can subscribe to your channel and get updated once new videos are released. Your channel profile will feature information about you, videos you've uploaded, subscribers, and comments. If you subscribe and comment on other people's channel pages, it will help spread word of your channel to others (in this way it's similar to a blog). You can customize your channel page by going into "My Account" and "Channel Settings." I've used YouTube to share yoga sequences, updates on our studio build-out, behind-the-scenes videos of photo shoots, and how-to-wear videos for items in my TranquiliT line. A basic digital camera or video camera will provide you with quality videos to share and promote your business.

SAVVY SOURCE FOR FURTHER EXPLORATION

YouTube: An Insider's Guide to Climbing the Charts, by Alan Lastufka and Michael W. Dean

Host a Teleclass

A teleclass is a wonderful way to connect with your clients. It's free to set up, easy to use, and all you need is a phone to make it happen. I recommend that you participate in a few teleclasses to see how they run before hosting your own. If you plan to offer an hour of musing, or an interview where you don't want background noise, you can mute the callers. Be sure to unmute during Q and A time, and don't mute yourself — I did that once and it's humiliating!

SAVVY SOURCE FOR FURTHER EXPLORATION

Freeconferencecall.com

Prepare notes, avoid reading directly from a script, and let the lecture flow, or make it fully interactive and simply pose a question that the callers comment on. I've seen teleclasses range from thirty minutes to a few hours in length, and tuition from free to one hundred dollars. Explore a few different formats, prices, times, and lengths to find your best fit. If you offer to record the teleclass as an MP3 and send it out to subscribers who can't join at that specific time, you increase your potential for reaching more people. I had a soldier call in from Iraq for one of my teleclasses and was in awe at her tenacity — it was 4 AM her time! Teleclasses offer a chance to touch many people.

141

Produce a Podcast

A podcast is a radio program that people download and listen to at their leisure. I started the *Tranquility du Jour* podcast in September 2005 and have produced over 150 shows. They are complimentary and available through iTunes and my blog, and have a per-episode listenership of approximately five thousand from around the globe. The show consists of interviews with fellow authors or other creative women, musings by *moi* on the yoga lifestyle, yoga poses, and how-tos.

Start with a blog — it's the backbone of the show, because it's where people will go to get the podcast or more information based on the podcast. Be strategic about your podcast: Who is the audience? Are there enough topics within your genre to keep the show going? How often will you put out new shows? How long will each one be? Answering these questions before you jump into the podcasting pool will make a big difference down the line.

Create an outline of your podcast, or your "show notes" — even the most skilled hosts use notes to keep them on track. Don't go overboard with equipment. Many computers have a microphone built in, and when combined with free Audacity software, you can begin recording and editing your shows for next to nothing! After you get proficient in editing and mixing, consider upgrading to a nicer microphone. Believe it or not, you can get close to a professional sound for well under two hundred dollars. Record a few shows as trial runs and listen to them with a critical ear. Is this the show you want the world to hear? If you're not Ms. Techie, consider using a service like Libsyn to host and help distribute your show. If you're a little bolder, consider the PodPress plug-in for WordPress blogs. There are tons of great resources to help you figure out how to get your show out to the world, and even into iTunes.

SAVVY SOURCES FOR FURTHER EXPLORATION
Audacity.sourceforge.net
Libsyn.com
Podcasting for Dummies, by Tee Morris and Evo Terra

142

Write Press Releases

The first time I pulled together a press release was for the launch of TranquiliT. For some reason I thought it was a terribly newsworthy event, and I made up darling media packets that I sent to ten major glossies, including *Glamour* and *O*. As you may imagine, I received no response. Then I did a bit more research and realized that Oprah wasn't on the edge of her seat waiting to discover what I was doing so that she could feature it. Pitching a press release is similar to pitching a story to a magazine: you have to know who you are pitching to and tailor the press release to them. Press releases are ways to share with the media your news about events, new products or services, new employees, do-gooding efforts, or awards.

HOW TO PEN A PRESS RELEASE

1. List "FOR IMMEDIATE RELEASE" in the upper left-hand corner.
2. Write a catchy headline in ALL CAPS.
3. Note the date and your city.
4. Capture the reader's attention with a lead sentence that clarifies what is happening.
5. Give the scintillating scoop in the first paragraph and elaborate in the following paragraph.
6. Be sure to note who, what, where, when, why, and how.
7. Include contact information so the media can get more details, or reference your website.
8. End with "###" so it's clear the press release is complete.
9. Be clear and concise, and keep the press release to one page.

Put Together a Media Kit

A media kit is a packet of information about your business that you pass along to the press. Items to have available and to include in the kit are FAQs, a listing of your products and services, a fact sheet outlining your history, a bio of the owner(s), current news, and media clips from former press features. Pull this kit together in a way that complements your brand and stands out — a bold folder with a branded sticker on front, or a recycled box with a branded tag if you want to include a product. Include things such as fabric swatches (if you're a designer) or cookies (if you're a baker) to make an impact. Be creative and have fun with this process. Your brand is, after all, a reflection of you.

Collect Media Clips

As you get recognition (even in a small company's newsletter), turn it into a press clip and highlight it on your website, in your store, or on your wall. Some press mentions are definitely bigger than others, but it is worth highlighting every mention you get when you're starting out. Once you've accumulated a bit of press, you can be more discriminating about what you display.

SAVVY SOURCE FOR FURTHER EXPLORATION

Sell Yourself Without Selling Your Soul: A Woman's Guide to Promoting Herself, Her Business, Her Product, or Her Cause with Integrity and Spirit, by Susan Harrow

Print a colorful eight-by-ten copy of a press clipping and frame it for display at your checkout counter. Include clips in your newsletter. Display an art book with your clips attached by old-fashioned corner seals. Laminate a color copy of a clipping and hang it from a ribbon with a clothespin. Add a press section to your website where you feature all the press you receive.

PROMOTIONS

There are simple ways to publicize your business, support your community, and leave a legacy through your work. If no one knows you exist, it's hard to make a difference. Following is a list of my favorite ways to plant seeds that will help your business bloom.

Designate Appreciation Weeks

One of my favorite promotions that we've been running for years is "Yogi Appreciation Week." We do these three times a year and offer 10 percent off all class passes and boutique purchases. Can you translate this to your own business and do something similar? You could host days (or even months) where you appreciate your clients by offering them rewards. Of course you would never take them for granted, but offering a special savings or event from time to time is a great way to nurture the relationship.

Put on Events

Throw special events to recognize your clients or to entice new ones: open houses, holiday parties, anniversary parties, or religious celebrations. The key to a successful event is choosing a catchy theme, getting the word out, and giving people a reason to come. Enticing reasons include free classes, goody bags, contributions to a charity, yummy food and drinks, free chair massages, featured artists or speakers, music, or special savings coupons. Try a special shopping day where everything is discounted. If your business is online, you can offer an online code that will let your clients save money. Offer something special to the first fifty people who come — always helpful to ensure early attendance. For our flagship studio's latest grand-opening event, we had a beautiful seedling tree wrapped in burlap with a branded tag tied with a bow for the first one hundred attendees.

145

Offer Refer-a-Friend Savings

Professionals of all types can benefit from a "refer a friend" offering, because people love to share good finds. If you provide a way for your clients to benefit from helping you spread the word, they may see this as an even greater incentive to share your excellent work. In addition, it's important to track where your new clients are coming from and how they hear about you, and to reward accordingly. If you find multiple clients being referred by a particular organization or individual, reach out and express your gratitude. We offer a free yoga class to any student who refers a friend who buys a class pass. You could offer a discount to any client who refers a client, or give a free gift (like a branded organic cotton T-shirt). These small incentives help spread your good tidings and give positive reinforcement along the way.

Send *Notes de Merci*

Thank-you notes are critical for any entrepreneur. Courtesy is not optional. Reach out to your supporters on a regular basis with a thank-you note sent via snail mail. Even thank-yous via text or email can be a breath of fresh air in our fast-paced society. When I worked retail during college, I would always send thank-yous to shoppers with my business card enclosed to encourage them to remember me. If you send a thank-you as a follow-up, it's nice to enclose something special, such as a tea bag, coupon, ticket to a special event, or trinket of some sort. You can expand the special experience you are trying to create beyond the interaction through this thoughtful gesture.

Showcase Your Goods

146

If you are in the service industry, I encourage you to add a product to your offerings. Start small. I began with printed tees for my yoga studio. Find a distributor of blank eco-friendly T-shirts, such as Alternative Apparel, and a local printing company. Pass along your logo or printer-ready image for the front and/or back. Voilà, you now have your own line of T-shirts. If you are a jewelry designer, never be seen without your creations. If you are a knitter, wear your scarves. This aligns with the notion of being your brand.

SAVVY SOURCE FOR FURTHER EXPLORATION
Alternativeapparel.com

Launch a Product

1. Determine what you want to produce. Sounds simple enough. Ask yourself: what is missing in the market that you'd like to have yourself? All of my businesses have started from a desire to have something (a nurturing yoga studio, yoga lifestyle wear, media about the yoga lifestyle, a holistic nonprofit for girls) that

didn't yet exist. Know your market and keep a particular muse in mind for your creation.

2. Find a supplier. Locate a wholesale distributor of the goods that you need in order to make the product.

3. Find a producer. You may want to launch a clothing line but don't have sewing genes. It's key that you find a professional to pull your product off brilliantly. Searching Craigslist or the Internet in general can be a helpful tool. If you're the producer of your product, make sure you're setting aside time to hone your craft so that you're able to continually improve and innovate.

SAVVY SOURCE FOR FURTHER EXPLORATION

Craigslist.org

4. Consult an attorney. You may need a patent, or there may be specific safety laws regarding your industry that are best to know up front.

147

5. Set a budget. Costs for supplies and production can easily get out of hand before you even get your product to market. Lay out costs based on supplier and production pricing. Determine how much you are willing to put into the product at the onset, and avoid going past that amount without serious soul-searching.

6. Make prototypes. Expect to make a few versions of the sample before perfection emerges. Avoid promising a release date without padding it substantially. Approve the final prototype only after you are 99 percent pleased. Have samples ready to show potential buyers.

7. Brand your product. Determine a catchy name for the product. Choose your colors, logo, and packaging. Find the perfect model for your look, and do a

photo shoot to showcase the product. Shoot detail and full-product shots. Design a website or add the line to an existing website. Create postcards, a catalogue, or promo materials. Pull together a story — tell who you are, why you created this, who it helps, and how. Give back by planting a tree for every online order you ship, contributing a portion of product sales to a charity, and donating your product to silent auctions or communities in need.

8. Sell your product. You need order forms and line sheets (which furnish a description of your product, pricing, colors, and sizes) to present to store buyers. Participate in industry-related trade shows — gift shows, clothing shows, and accessory shows — and sell to shop owners or directly to the public. Host a trunk show and invite all your friends; encourage them to bring friends. If you're ready to sell wholesale (at half of your retail price), call local boutiques, ask to speak with the buyer, and set up an appointment to show your product. Send your marketing materials to boutiques around the country that you think would be a good fit for your product. Be sure to follow up. Selling on consignment is a great option if you want to test the market with a buyer who isn't willing to invest in it yet. The store will pay you when the product sells, giving you 40 to 60 percent of retail value. A great option if the buyer is teetering on the verge of writing an order. There's no risk on the store's part, and your consignment sales can show them how well your product will do with their clients. If your product is handmade, set up an Etsy.com account. Set up an online merchant account. You must be able to sell online, even if you start with a

PayPal account rather than a full-fledged merchant account, which means oodles of paperwork. Set up shipping accounts (USPS.com, UPS.com, Fedex.com), and get recycled shipping products (mailers, tissue paper, bubble wrap) if you'll be mailing your goods to wholesalers or online shoppers. Choose green options when possible, and create little waste.

SAVVY SOURCE FOR FURTHER EXPLORATION

Craft, Inc.: Turn Your Creative Hobby into a Business, by Meg Mateo Ilasco

Recognize a Client, Vendor, Retailer, Charity, and Team Member of the Month

Recognizing a contributor to your business and featuring this person in a special way builds community, rewards good behavior, and increases morale. Take a photo of this contributor, post his or her name, ask for a testimonial and share it in your newsletter, name a product or menu offering after this person, highlight his or her story on your website, or give the person a gift or a special parking spot. Building and nurturing relationships as you grow will do so much for you as an individual and an organization. Everyone craves acknowledgment and kudos, and, as a business owner, I recommend you do all you can to make those around you feel special.

149

Set Up an Amazon aStore

If you find yourself constantly recommending certain products, books, or music to your clients, you can make a tiny commission for your efforts by setting up an Amazon aStore. To get started, go to aStore.amazon.com and follow the instructions. I constantly get requests for suggested yoga DVDs, books, or music, and I find this tool helpful for assisting my yogis in finding what they need. If you have a few people on your team, why not create a page for each of them so that your clients can see your team's staff picks? At bookstores, I always find myself drawn to the staff picks, and I believe our clients like to know what's on our playlists and our bookshelves.

BUILDING AN EMPIRE

Play with the marketing ideas that most appeal to you. Try to do one small thing every day that shares your start-up with the world — write a blog post, donate a gift certificate to a good cause, pen a thank-you note, add to your product line or Amazon store, host a special event, speak to a women's group, produce a podcast, tweet tiny inspirations, set out promo cards at a local café, or teach a workshop. Enjoy this journey, and let your creativity shine.

MODEL MUSE

Eileen Fisher began her clothing empire with $350 and a dream. Now her products are sold in department stores, and she has forty-two stand-alone stores. Women are drawn to her comfortable, simple designs, which transition from work to everyday wear. Named among the top twenty-five best medium-sized companies to work in, her company emphasizes a balance between work and life for her team. The company's website highlights their leadership practices: keep it simple, inspire creativity, engage people, communicate openly, nurture growth in others, nurture growth in yourself, team with people, communicate our vision, tell the truth, and communicate a joyful atmosphere. Eileen does all of this with a focus on social consciousness through sustainability, community partnerships, support for women, and human rights. Her campaigns feature women of all ages and nationalities. Meditation and yoga are close to her heart, and she also offers an annual scholarship to women growing a business. This woman is the epitome of building a business in a mindful, profitable, genuine way. Learn more at Eileenfisher.com.

8. EMPOWERED EXPANSION

*And the day came when the risk to remain tight in a bud
was more painful than the risk it took to blossom.*

— ANAÏS NIN

As you and your business continue to grow, there are new skills to hone and bridges to cross. Exciting and scary all rolled together. In this section we'll explore creating your dream team, diversifying your offerings, financing your growth, and building green. Let the games begin!

YOUR DREAM TEAM

There may come a time when you realize you can't do everything. Shocking, yes. When you're ready to take the leap into being a boss, it's a whole new world of responsibility and requires a skill set very different from that of the entrepreneur. In this section I'll unveil enlightened ways to hire, manage, and reward your team. Getting the right team on board is essential to your health and well-being. Where to start?

Make a list of what you are currently doing, as an entrepreneur, that is not a good use of your time. Filing paperwork. Following up with clients who haven't paid. Website maintenance. Editing. Shipping orders. Managing inventory. Cleaning. Invoicing clients. Ordering supplies. Merchandising. Sending intake forms to new clients. Managing your schedule. Making travel arrangements. Designing promotional materials. Doing photo shoots. Inputting data into QuickBooks. Paying bills. Setting and overseeing budgets. The list of to-dos for running a business is endless.

Once you determine what you spend time on that is not fulfilling or otherwise a good use of your creative spark, let's get clear on the help that you may need. If you are concerned about the financials or logistics involved in hiring someone to help, you can always start with a part-time assistant or temporary help (for example, a gift wrapper to get you through the holidays). Clarify what you need so you can start the arduous and oh-so-important hiring process. To begin, draft a job description for this new position that lays out the title, working environment, who the employee will report to (you!), overall responsibility, pay (you're a small business owner, and this helps prevent the expectation of a corporate salary), perks (for example, casual setting, pet-friendly venue, monthly manis) plus skill, education, and experience qualifications. Convey the culture you want to cultivate: creative, corporate, or somewhere in between. Consult your attorney or accountant to determine if the new hire will be classified as an independent contractor (who pays his or her own taxes) or employee (you pay the taxes).

Now you're ready to share the position with the world by posting it online, on your website, and on your blog. Request cover letters and résumés. Share the news with your networks and mailing lists. Request that the recipients pass it along to anyone they think would be interested and let you know if they have the perfect candidate in mind. Personal referrals are great resources for your building a dream team.

How to Hire

Begin collecting résumés and cover letters. A cover letter makes or breaks my interest in a candidate. By examining what they share in their cover letters, you can tell those who have done their research,

SAMPLE JOB DESCRIPTION

Assistant to the Director

This exciting position involves customer service/front desk/ retail sales and a wide range of administrative tasks, including events coordination, errand-running, and written communication. Day-to-day duties include managing studio calendar, handling incoming email and voicemail, ensuring studios are clean and well stocked, managing class sign-ins, and handling retail sales. This role requires the ability to prioritize, brainstorm, and gracefully handle issues as they arise.

Organization, reliability, creativity, attention to detail, excellent written and verbal communication skills, and the ability to multitask are absolute musts. This position is great for lovers of yoga and a wonderful learning experience for those interested in running their own businesses. Hours are 9 am–3 pm Monday–Friday. Compensation is $12 per hour, unlimited yoga, 25 percent discount off all studio offerings, and the opportunity to help create the future of Tranquil Space. To apply, send your résumé and a cover letter outlining why you want to work with us.

know about your organization, and feel like a good fit before even looking at their résumés. Contact the potential candidates, and set up a phone interview to start. At times, I've gotten overly excited about a candidate and made an in-person interview the first step, and then come away wanting my hour back. So, think of it as a date — do drinks (or a quick chat on the phone) before the four-course dinner. This will let you get a vibe from the candidate and determine whether or not to bring her in for a second interview. Let candidates know your time line. As a courtesy, if you don't plan on calling for a second interview, send an email thanking her for her time, and let her know that you are pursuing other candidates.

During the second interview you can give her a tour of your space, introduce her to any other key players in your organization, let them ask her some questions (even if they are friends of yours or advisory board members), and get a better feel for whether she will fit into your culture. It's helpful to get additional input, since the wrong hire can have drama-filled ramifications.

SAMPLE INTERVIEW QUESTIONS
(IN NO PARTICULAR ORDER)

What makes you a good candidate for this position/fit for this organization?

At your previous jobs, how did you fill downtime?

Tell me about your last job performance review. Kudos? Room for improvement?

If you had a question and I wasn't around to answer it, how would you resolve it?

What do you know about my company? Have you sampled its products or services?

Is there anything that could prevent you from consistently being on time and putting in a full day's work?

What did you most enjoy about your last job? Least enjoy?

How would you respond to an upset customer?

Give an example of when you went above and beyond what was expected of you in your previous position.

Rate your candidates and narrow the field down to your top two or three. Check their references. If necessary, have one more phone interview to ask any remaining questions and discuss a training time line. A narrowing factor between two candidates could be something as small as their availability to fit your training and starting time line, or how they respond to one final request to answer a few more questions. Getting the right person on board, especially as your first hire, is incredibly important and will help set the tone for future hires.

Once you've made your decision, call the candidate and offer her the position. This is usually an exciting moment for you both. Let her know that an offer letter and agreement will be forthcoming (give her your time line), confirm your schedule and her starting date, and get prepared for the next step . . . training!

The offer letter lays out your enthusiastic offer: job description, salary, benefits, vacation and sick time, expenses (if applicable), plus starting date, time, and location. Include a separate attachment for your employee (or independent contractor) agreement. This document is best drafted by an attorney and includes information on taxes, noncompetition, and nonsolicitation. It also notes that the new hire is an at-will employee, outlines the services she will be providing, and clarifies corporate culture and dress code, confidentiality, compensation, return of company property, and a bunch of basic legalese. As a former paralegal, I'm diligent about this step, and I highly encourage you to get everything in writing to avoid any misunderstanding in the future. Your local small business association may also be able to assist with forms and basic logistics as you set out to grow your organization from a sole proprietorship to a mini empire.

Tranquil Training

As a first-time manager or an experienced one, you'll find that taking the time to properly train and welcome your new hire helps set the tone for her experience with your organization. I like to give welcoming gifts such as a branded organic cotton T-shirt, goody bag, or special lunch. The initial training experience is full of paperwork: signing the employment/contractor agreement, payroll documents, W2 form (for employees), W4 form (for independent contractors), I-9 (employment eligibility), and state tax forms (for employees). Once you get through those boring but essential logistics, the walk-through of the job description details takes place.

Go through each of the items outlined in the job description, bring her up to speed on current priorities and projects, assign tasks, and set up a communication tool through which you will both stay connected.

One of my favorite online communication tools is Backpack (Backpackit.com). I have found it very helpful for staying connected on goals, daily action items, research, passwords, how-tos, links to suppliers, and more. An online system such as Backpack or PBworks (Pbwiki.com) gives you an easily editable employee manual and communication tool for your team to access wherever Internet is available. Using these online systems helps ensure that much-needed documents are not on only one physical computer.

During the training period, discuss what you expect from the new employee — namely, details concerning email turnaround time, status updates, meetings, dress code, work schedule, overtime, breaks, requests for weekly reports with status of projects, and personal Internet and phone usage. Don't rely on one day of training to be the end-all, be-all, however. Continually reinforce the training and give ongoing reminders, because a person's attention span and ability to absorb what you share at any given time is only so large.

Team Management

Keep your staff motivated, encouraged, and in the know. Show your team you care by offering tokens of gratitude (see the "Tokens of Gratitude" sidebar for ideas) and kudos. Address concerns as they arise, and give formal feedback through three-month and annual performance reviews. Clearly define areas where your staff can improve, and then follow up by taking whatever actions are needed. Have a corrective action feedback form where you outline the impact of individual team members' actions on the organization. If the situation does not improve after a few formal discussions, you must cut your losses. Sad, but true.

Do what you can to help develop your employees' personal and professional goals. Invest in your team's development by sending them to classes or workshops to expand their skill sets. Hold regular meetings and provide updates on projects, priorities, and procedures. This also allows for a regular forum where you and your employees can express any issues or concerns that may be brewing. Assign tasks with clear instructions and deadlines. Have an open-door policy and be available to answer questions or offer assistance. Regularly review and update job descriptions in a collaborative manner with your team. Be a role model. Use your communication tools regularly, so your team will stay connected and updated on the goings-on. Share your schedule with your team so they know what you do. Handle negative feedback or issues immediately. Don't fall into the trap of wanting everyone to like you — management is not a popularity contest.

SAVVY SOURCE FOR FURTHER EXPLORATION

The Girl's Guide to Being a Boss (without Being a Bitch): Valuable Lessons, Smart Suggestions, and True Stories for Succeeding as the Chick-in-Charge, by Caitlin Friedman and Kimberly Yorio

157

TOKENS OF GRATITUDE

Make sure your team feels appreciated by sending kudos-filled emails, offering special discount days, giving small gifts, saying "thank you," publicly acknowledging their efforts, highlighting a team player, remembering their birthdays, letting them leave early on a sunny or snowy day, bringing snacks to a meeting, treating them to a meal, helping them develop professionally, assisting with envelope stuffing or cleaning up after a big event, throwing them a special soiree, and giving them gift cards to their favorite tea spots.

Team Retreats

Get your team together in a comfortable setting and in a format different from that of a typical meeting to take the pulse of your organization and exercise your leadership muscles. I've done small management retreats with senior managers on my team where we got pedicures, set goals for the next quarter, checked in on how things were flowing, created wish lists, shared a meal, and designed action steps for moving forward.

I've also facilitated larger team retreats for other organizations where we created a mission statement, did yoga together, evaluated individual levels of personal satisfaction, set group goals, discussed challenges within the smaller groups and the team as a whole, and came away with a plan for our next steps. For my studio's annual team retreat (which can encompass seventy team members from our three locations), I have brought in speakers, hosted an ecofashion show, meditated, discussed the big picture, and had department or studio leaders give updates while we nibbled on vegetarian treats. The opportunity to step away from ringing phones and email to focus strategically for a few hours can have profound effects on team morale and overall productivity.

If your team is you and one other person, it's still necessary to check in regularly. Treating your team member to lunch, checking in on the state of affairs and her level of satisfaction, and setting bigger-picture goals can help infuse your culture with team spirit and strategic understanding. If you have a larger team, it is even more critical that you host regular gatherings where everyone can connect. Some organizations are run on shifts, and your staff may feel like ships passing in the night. Meeting for a retreat gives everyone a chance to reconnect and builds camaraderie.

Determine your goal as the leader of the organization. What do you want to see happen during and as a result of this meeting? Do you want to rebrand? Come up with new product, program, or service ideas? Address a point of tension? Inspire? Train? Build community? Give kudos? Identify issues? Set standards? Define goals? Update others on the state of affairs? Share your vision and get input? Assess performance based on previous goals? You're a go-getter, so you may want to do all of the above!

Get clear on the focus of the team retreat, and adjust your agenda accordingly. Give the agenda to your team in advance and give them "omwork" so they come prepared to address the topic or topics at hand. Host the event in a setting outside your office, if possible, and provide tasty treats. Everyone loves to nosh. Providing some sort of gift or goody bag for your team is also a lovely touch. If you're not comfortable with facilitating, bring in an outside facilitator who is well versed in your organization, or an outside speaker who can give insight into a topic you'll be covering.

SAVVY SOURCE FOR FURTHER EXPLORATION

See Jane Lead: 99 Ways for Women to Take Charge at Work, by Lois P. Frankel

159

Once the retreat is over, provide follow-up and next steps. It's key to ensure that your team knows they were heard, so indicate this in your response. In your follow-up note, you can also share photos from the event, offer any special thank-yous, and express gratitude to the whole team for their efforts in growing your organization. Team retreats entail a lot of planning, facilitating, and follow-up, but they will help make your organization and team members shine.

COMMUNITY EFFORTS

For you, the business owner, your community consists of the people you serve, people in your surrounding area whom you don't yet serve, fellow business owners, and colleagues in your industry. If you're online, your community may even be global. Staying connected and giving back is the way to ensure you continue to practice enlightened work. Welcome an incoming business, give kudos to a colleague who has won an award, and hold special events for your clients and open houses to welcome in your not-yet-clients. Invite your competition to lunch. Mingle with your local politicos and keep them abreast of your organization's efforts. Send flowers to help celebrate a nearby business's special event. Befriend industry names on Facebook. Follow them on Twitter. Reach out to colleagues in your sphere and make connections. These people will become part of your dream team as supporters, and this will bring great karma to you as a business owner.

Diversify

As your organizational baby moves from infancy to toddlerhood, it's important to explore ways to diversify your portfolio. Relying on one client, product, supplier, or service to sustain you through thick and thin is not savvy. Especially in a challenging economy, your biggest client may run into financial trouble, and if you're relying on that client or one piece of your business to sustain you, you may find yourself in a tough situation. As with financial investments, don't put all your eggs in one basket. Following are some suggestions on how to diversify. You're sure to find a new passion or talent along the way.

Be a Diversification Diva

You may be thinking: "I'm already exhausted and barely able to handle my current workload, and now you're saying I should do more?" Yes, I am. Not only is diversification a smart business decision, but it can also give you a new jolt of energy. At times, handling the same issues day in, day out, can take a toll. By adding something new to the mix, you get to use different parts of your brain, connect with your creative spirit, and get reenergized with

TIME LINE OF MY DIVERSIFICATION

1999: Launch Tranquil Space in living room.

2000: Move Tranquil Space to church parlor.

2002: Launch TranquiliT clothing line and Tranquil Space teacher training. Host first international retreat and release *Vinyasa Yoga with Kimberly Wilson* audio CD.

2003: Move Tranquil Space to two-level new home and release *Vinyasa Yoga for the Newbie Yogi* audio CD.

2004: Launch blog and Tranquil Space Bethesda.

2005: Launch podcast.

2006: Launch Tranquil Space Foundation, publish *Hip Tranquil Chick: A Guide to Life On and Off the Yoga Mat*, release *Get Your Yoga On* audio CD.

2007: Launch Tranquil Space Arlington and start column for the *Washington Examiner*.

2008: Move Tranquil Space to ecofabulous three-level home with spa, tea bar, boutique, and studios.

2009: Host ten-year Tranquil Space birthday bash and release *Tranquility to Go* audio CD.

2010: Publish *Tranquilista: Mastering the Art of Enlightened Work and Mindful Play*.

the challenge of something new. Here's a list of ways to become a diversifying diva in your business:

- Add a complementary product (example: add pants to your dress collection).
- Introduce a complementary service (example: add reflexology to your massage options).
- Add a new location (example: expand to a nearby neighborhood or city).
- Target another market (example: add maternity options to your collection).
- Franchise or license your business.

- Form alliances with like-minded organizations.
- Teach classes, workshops, or retreats.
- Write magazine articles or a column.
- Break into the paid speaking circuit.
- Merge with or acquire a company.
- Go online (example: offer products online in addition to maintaining your retail store).
- Rent out your space when you're not using it.
- Produce and sell a CD, DVD, or MP3.
- Offer teleclasses.

The trick with diversifying is not spreading yourself too thin or getting into unrelated revenue streams. For example, if you are a holistic health counselor, adding a tanning bed to your menu would not align with your core offering. Also, it can get exciting to try new things, but if you're not able to sleep at night because of lack of time and energy, it's best to rethink large expansions. There is no science to this process. It is truly an art, and a very individual one. Start with one diversification and see how it feels. Then continue to add more diversifications, depending on your energy, feedback from clients, and what most resonates with you.

I find that my diversified portfolio offers me a shift in roles that I enjoy: it can be exhilarating to dash from teaching yoga to choosing colors for next season's TranquiliT line, to nominating a charity for one of the Tranquil Space Foundation's microgrants, to recording a podcast. However, I've read that, from a time-management perspective, it is best to wear one hat at a time, rather than bouncing among your diversified interests by multitasking. Ideally choose days or even half days where you focus on one of the various parts of your business, to prevent feeling overwhelmed and as if you have multiple personalities.

FINANCING GROWTH

As you know, I'm a "start small, grow organically" kind of gal. I started the studio, my first business, using money made from my thirty-one-thousand-dollar-a-year job. My flagship studio financed my diversified additions, such as the clothing line and additional locations. By loaning money to the new ventures, I didn't have to deal with a bank or apply for loans and was able to test the waters relatively risk-free. I didn't take out a business loan until I needed a huge amount to finance our build-out. The loan process took a couple of months and was a tedious, paperwork-intensive journey with the Small Business Association.

A few years ago a local bank sent me a promo offering a line of credit and waiving its annual fee. I decided to apply since it didn't cost anything and would help protect the studio in case of emergency. I went on to apply for a second one at my main bank, and these two lines of credit saved me during a build-out process that ran 50 percent over its projected cost.

I'm fairly risk-averse and have taken small, strategic, calculated steps over the years. Getting into debt to take the studio to the next level was a scary endeavor, especially considering the economic downturn of 2008. However, I don't regret the process, am proud that I didn't need financing before year eight, and only wish the build-out hadn't gone over its budget so substantially. You may be wondering how to take your business to the next level by opening another location or adding a product to your existing offerings. Here are suggestions on how to make your decision carefully:

SECURE A LINE OF CREDIT. You may not need it now, but you'll be grateful you have it when you do need it. This is a flexible option and allows you to take a small amount, rather than the lump sum (like a loan), as you need it.

KEEP YOUR CASH FLOW FLOWING. It's best to have at least six months in reserve to cover basics such as payroll, rent, and utilities.

APPLY FOR A FIXED-RATE LOAN. If you need money for a build-out or expansion, applying for a loan offers you the chance to borrow a certain amount and repay it in fixed monthly installments.

ESTABLISH A RELATIONSHIP WITH YOUR BANK. Connecting with the tellers and management ensures you're not just another application when you need their assistance.

MAKE A BUDGET AND EVALUATE IT MONTHLY. Once you've been in business for a year, you will have a basic understanding of your expenses. Sure, these will be in flux as you add additional staff or sundries, but it's helpful to have a baseline to work from. Set up a monthly budget that outlines your expenses, and do your best to stay within the budget. If you need additional supplies one month, try to make up for the overage by underspending in another category. This basic tool helps you allocate your funds intentionally.

DETERMINE WHAT YOU REALLY NEED. As my business needs and profits have shifted, I've adjusted my earnings accordingly. When I started the business, I budgeted what I needed to survive (for example, rent/mortgage, groceries, utilities, insurance). I've done the same thing during our leaner times, adjusting my income to cover only my necessities. If you know what your bottom line is, it will help ease panic when certain months (or years) are not meeting your projections.

SAVVY SOURCE FOR FURTHER EXPLORATION
Mint.com

Add Locations

Daunting, yes, but read on! There may come a time when you're ready to add a second location, or an opportunity presents itself that you decide to explore. As I've moved locations over the years, it's been to secure larger space to accommodate growth. The additional locations have been a way to offer yoga in nearby markets. Before taking the leap into a new space, here is a checklist to ensure you're ready.

- Is your current location generating a profit and running smoothly?
- Will you manage the new space from your current location or have an office in the new location?
- Do you have the time and energy to manage multiple locations?
- Will this add value for your target market?
- Have you received multiple requests to launch this new location/venture?
- Do you have the staff necessary to tend it?
- Can you afford to test this new location? I encourage starting with a short-term lease to sample the waters.
- How long do you plan to give the new location before determining whether it's a good fit?

Maintain your quality of life while you are building your business. If, after reflecting on the above questions, you determine it isn't the right time to move forward with a new location, it doesn't mean that this will be the case in six months. You have to be willing to walk away from certain opportunities that don't feel like the perfect fit at the time. You're not closing the door forever, just while you stabilize and get through whatever else is on your plate.

Build It Green

Designing a new space is incredibly exciting and overwhelming. When determining the look and feel for my recent build-out, I coined the term *Zen princess*. I wanted a look that oozed simplicity and spaciousness, but which also had splashes of girly flair. And I wanted to build it as "green" as possible by using recycled materials, rather than letting them be sent to landfills as I bought new "green" ones. Within Tranquil Space you'll find the following:

- Bamboo, cork, stained concrete, and wood from an old barn as flooring
- Two walls covered with wood from an old farmhouse
- A dramatic chandelier that greets all who enter with warm, glittery light
- A feminine spa setting complete with fluffy rug, chandeliers, and reused settee and pocket doors
- A vintage skylight reused as a window
- Floor joists reused as shelving
- Damask wallpaper that covers patches of plastic near exposed brick
- Dressing stalls made out of the pallets that delivered construction supplies
- Reused metal tree grates, commonly seen in urban settings, to hold up the seating benches made of reclaimed barn wood
- Low-VOC (volatile organic compounds) paints in soothing hues, such as light lavender, slate gray, light yellow

Voilà! A perfect blending of both Zen and princess. Be creative when designing your space, as sometimes opposites work very well together and bring a sense of balance to your various preferences.

To get a vibe for the look you want to create, begin tearing images from magazines that appeal to you — colors, aesthetics, furnishings, fixtures, flooring, lighting. Assemble a collage with all the images, and a theme will emerge. This will help you determine how to pull it all together. Being the green goddess that you are, of course you want to create a space that has a small carbon footprint, so I have some suggestions to offer.

Flooring

There are many eco options out there, and the choice may be overwhelming. If wood is what you're seeking, try to find reclaimed wood or wood with the Forest Stewardship Council's stamp of approval, to ensure that the wood you purchased came from a well-managed forest. Another great green option is bamboo (but be forewarned that it can be very soft if you have a stiletto-wearing crowd) and cork. To get a unique look, stain concrete with a water-based stain and low-VOC polish.

167

Energy

Before we moved in, we had to replace all the windows in our new location due to years of wear and tear. Although it was very pricey, I'm certain the new windows are saving us a lot by preventing heating and cooling from literally going out the window. Install energy-efficient windows to help keep heat and cold where you want them. Skylights can also be a great source of light and heat during the day. Look into wind-powered energy options in your area. We were able to switch to 100 percent wind-powered energy through a local organization called Clean Currents. Forgo incandescent bulbs and instead use compact fluorescents. Some businesses have lights that are hardwired to stay on 24/7. If yours are, make sure you use bulbs with a high Energy Star rating.

Walls

Use low-VOC paints to protect not only the environment but also your team and clients. If you're using wallpaper, avoid vinyl

SAVVY SOURCE FOR FURTHER EXPLORATION
Wallwords.com

varieties and look for sources for natural papers or organic fabrics. You can create a textured look with sponges dipped in paint, or even faux marbling, by using low-VOC paints. Another option is to stencil your logo or inspirational words on walls and doors.

Loo

Look for the fancy, Euro dual-flush toilet options — one button uses more water, one button uses less water. Educate users with a sign noting which button uses more and which uses less. They'll figure out the reasoning without your having to spell it out. Provide alternatives to paper towels, such as small, rolled-up cloths that you can launder, or high-speed, energy-efficient hand dryers.

Furnishings

Check out secondhand stores in your area to furnish your new space. I've discovered great finds such as couches, chairs, desks, and bookshelves at these stores and flea markets. With a little paint, TLC, and my penchant for shabby chic style, these items proved to be the perfect fit (and price) for me. Determine what you need, and search for alternative options to fulfill your list. Peruse estate sales, Freecycle.com, and Craigslist.org for additional offbeat, economical, and green options to outfit your business. Don't overlook the water-stained couch or paint-chipped cabinets. Adding a fluffy blanket over the couch or fresh coat of paint to the cabinets may bring them back to life.

ENLIGHTENED EXPANSION

As you and your business grow, you have an even larger opportunity to touch more people. The ability to touch another's life is an incredible gift. Building a business grants us this gift every single day. Hire wisely. Nurture your team. Diversify your port-folio. Save for a rainy day. And build green!

MODEL MUSE

The pink-Cadillac lady who lived in a pink house in Dallas, Texas, is the featured muse of expansion. Frustrated by being passed over for a promotion by a man she trained, Mary Kay Ash began her cosmetics company as a single mother with five thousand dollars. She built an empire through direct selling, empowering women, and encouraging a strong connection to family based on the golden rule. *Fortune* magazine recognized the company as one of the hundred best companies to work for in the United States. Mary Kay believed in the unlimited potential of women — a belief her mother had instilled in her. Her leadership style has been touted in numerous books, and she founded the Mary Kay Ash Charitable Foundation with a mission to end violence against women and cancers affecting women. Learn more at Marykay.com.

169

FINALE

Your playing small doesn't serve the world. There's nothing enlightened about shrinking so that other people won't feel insecure around you. We are all meant to shine, as children do.

— MARIANNE WILLIAMSON

It has been my pleasure to take you down the tranquilista path. This simple road map will assist you on your journey to living life as brightly as possible — in full bloom. Take the ideas that most resonate with you, try a few that don't, and do all you can to live your life in a way that shines. The work starts within and radiates out. Your presence can have a profound impact on others and the world around you. Luxuriate in this experience by living out loud and leaving an inspiring legacy — all while rolling out your yoga mat and enjoying a yummy pot of organic chamomile tea. Life is meant to be savored.

I hope our paths will cross, and that this book will assist you in living a full life — complete with belly laughs and sprinkles on top. Stay connected to our virtual community through the Tranquility du Jour blog and podcast at Tranquilitydujour.com, *s'il vous plaît*. Join *moi* for a workshop, or consider jet-setting to an exotic locale for full-fledged retreat immersion in "tranquilology." Wherever your journey takes you, *merci beaucoup* for exploring the beauty of living a tranquility-filled life with me.

May your mark on this world be bold, bright, and beautiful!

Keep shining,

Kimberly

ACKNOWLEDGMENTS

Many divine souls helped make this book possible, including

My beau, Tim Mooney, who has the patience of Job and
an amazing sense of humor, and who is the best
cheerleader a girl could ask for.

My pup, Louis the Pug, for his never-ending snore, continual "burfs!" and unconditional love.

My mum, who throws the best book-signing soirees, is
my biggest fan, and planted the DIY bug in me at an
early age.

My pops, who has now read his second book catering
to women (*Hip Tranquil Chick* was his first), offered
oodles of editing input ("comma here, no comma
there"), and helped me launch my literary journey,
as a little girl, on his typewriter.

My agent, Jennifer Gates, who has been an avid supporter
since receiving my first query letter.

My editor, Georgia Hughes, who graciously showed me
around the lovely New World Library headquarters
and has been enthusiastic about this project.

New World Library, who welcomed me into their literary family.

The teams at Tranquil Space, TranquiliT, and Tranquil Space Foundation, who keep me motivated each and every day with their wit, spirit, and passion for spreading tranquility.

My friend Heather Haines, who generously gave lots of feedback on the birth of *Tranquilista*.

My podcast listeners, teleclass participants, retreat divas, and blog readers, who inspire me to do more, be more, and give more.

Trudy Hale, proprietor of the Porches Writing Retreat, where I clocked three divine weeks of writing time while immersed in the serenity of fall foliage and ice-covered trees, sans Internet.

INDEX

179

T

ABOUT THE AUTHOR

Kimberly Wilson is a teacher, writer, do-gooder, entrepreneur, and ecofashion designer. She is the creative director and founder of Tranquil Space — named among the top twenty-five yoga studios in the world by *Travel + Leisure* — and the author of *Hip Tranquil Chick*. She holds a master's degree in women's studies.

When she's not bookstore browsing, you'll find her sipping pots of tea, crafting new TranquiliT designs, or leading retreats globally. Her work has been featured on *Martha Stewart Living Radio*, and in *Daily Candy*, *Fit Yoga*, *U.S. News*, and *Shape*.

With a passion for do-gooding, Kimberly launched the Tranquil Space Foundation to assist women and girls in finding tranquility through yoga, creativity, and leadership, and is currently pursuing a master's degree in social work. She lives in a *petite* raspberry-colored flat in Washington, DC, with two fancy felines named after French impressionists, a supportive beau, and a black pug.

Indulge in ongoing musings in Kimberly's blog and podcast, Tranquility du Jour. Peruse Kimberlywilson.com.